Eyes Upward

Real-Life Stories to
Encourage You,
Challenge You,
and Make You
Laugh a Little, too...

NATASHA GRANTZ

Woven Books
YOUR STORY. HIS GLORY.

Woven Books, a division of Wonderfully Woven, LLC

YOUR STORY. HIS GLORY.

KDP ISBN: 9798339471554
Published in the United States of America October 2024
Content Editor: Lori Clapper, Woven Books
Book Cover: WP Pals
Layout & Design: Michelle Morrow. Publishology
Proofreader: Kristin Collins, The KC Creative
First edition 2024

Contents

Praise for Natasha Grantz

"Natasha wrote a book that we all need. She beautifully weaves the heart of God into each story. Her gift to pinpoint a spiritually rich meaning behind her shared circumstances is insightful. God's truth applied to her own brokenness gives us heaven-sent wisdom and is an inspiration to many. Her vulnerability and willingness to share her own woundedness is healing for the damaged soul. Her friendly and compassionate voice is read on every page. *Eyes Upward* is a compilation of stories that is easily shared with sojourners on our path towards the Savior. Her message of hope bridges the deep hurts of life with God's ever abundant mercy and grace."

Janelle Keith, Author Coach and Editor with Woven Books Publishing & Media Services; Author of *Grace For Your Waist: Living a Lifestyle Fitted With Hope; Shaped By Grace: Lose the Lies and Gain God's Truth Devotional; Shaped By Grace: Lose the Lies and Gain God's Truth Journal;* and (coming soon) *Grace For Your Pace: How to Burn On Instead of Burn Out.*

"Natasha does a great job sharing personal stories that we can all relate to and weaving in strong Biblical truths. Her use of humor makes it easy for us all to relate to the circumstances without feeling judged. Natasha is a woman's woman and uses her vulnerability to draw in the reader and give them hope. I would recommend this book to anyone that feels that they are alone and navigating life without a net. That net is Jesus."

Joy Trachsel, Speaker/Author/Pastoral Counselor
www.joytrachsel.com

"If you are struggling to put a finger on how God interacts with us, or have felt like He's not present with you, I recommend *Eyes Upward*. Natasha guides you by sharing her own life experiences as she has grown in her relationship with the Lord. She gives you eyes to recognize where He is acting in your everyday experiences, including the hard ones. I love her vulnerability and honesty. The format is accessible and perfect for meditating on the goodness and sovereignty of the Lord. I found hope, encouragement, and real-life applications in every story."

Kristin Collins, Owner of The KC Creative

To the late Mr. Fred Rogers,
a man whose life and legacy I greatly admire. May we
not only learn to love, teach, and value one another
(both children and adults) as he did, but may we become
intent listeners and "doers of the Word" as he was.
I'm looking forward to meeting you in Heaven one day,
sir. I know you'll have a lot to talk about, and I
will too...

EYES UPWARD

Dear Friend,

It was an absolute honor and privilege praying for you as I wrote the following pages. I thought of you during every step of the process. More importantly, I hope you know your Heavenly Daddy thinks of you *all* the time.

My prayer is that my honest life stories in this book will refresh and enhance your relationship with God in new and exciting ways.

No matter where you find yourself reading—whether on a park bench soaking up some sunshine or hiding on the toilet, trying to get a break from your kids—I hope you'll feel His love. I also hope you use the prompts at the end of each story. Just like anything else, you get out what you put into it.

Thank you for going on this journey with me as we seek to scoot a little closer to the lover of our souls.

Natasha

ONE

Feelin' Like a Leper

Like most people, I've had several close friends over the years. They were all very different from one another, but with each one of them, I laughed until I couldn't breathe more times than I can count. Thinking about the memories of all the silly things we did still makes me smile.

One of those friends and I bonded from the moment we met. Her cozy, well-decorated house felt like my second home. There was nothing like going there after school, knowing the refrigerator would greet us with string cheese or some other "gourmet" snack. Everything tastes better at your friend's house than it does at home, of course. As we grew up and eventually faced the transition from middle school to high school, our friendship fizzled. She was busy making new friends, as she was encouraged to no longer be friends with me (to put it bluntly), and I was busy seeking love and acceptance from boys. My soul's journey was disguised as promiscuity, and then … I got pregnant at 15.

It hurt me to lose that friendship, but what hurt even more was the *rejection* I felt behind it. Feelings of being unlovable and discarded bubbled up inside me, even though I didn't fully understand those emotions. To make matters worse, my family didn't have the kind of money and prominent reputations that my old friend's new circle had. Although my family is White, and I've had just as many White friends as Black, it also made me feel insecure about being biracial. This is because the girls who *did* "make the cut" were all White (just like my friend), and they possessed a certain personality type I didn't have. Naturally, it made me look at myself and compare. All I saw in the mirror was a girl who fell short; she simply wasn't good enough. Then to top it off, becoming a teen mom quickly upgraded me from "bad influence" to *stay even further away from her now–she has the plague.*

Rejection is devastating. This situation affected me for many years, somewhat subconsciously. As you may know, it can be rather difficult to recognize feelings (or a spirit) of rejection— let alone admit it and process it. Sometimes it manifests in the form of bitterness, anger, or jealousy. But when we take a good, honest look at our hearts and peel back all the layers, we'll often find a wound. Looking back, I don't fault this friend's parents one bit. They were simply protecting their girl in the best way they knew how, and I can respect that.

Sadly, the rejection didn't stop there. One of my biological parents, whom I had only met three years before getting pregnant, told my half siblings that I would be a failure for the rest of my life now. In fact, they were no longer allowed to remain in contact with me and faced very serious consequences when they tried to connect. My teen-mom situation was used as a teaching lesson, but not in a healthy or loving way. I felt like the black sheep. Although this was a professed "Christian" household, I felt everything *but* love. I was not only shunned, emotionally and physically, during that season, but they unapologetically bashed my adoptive parents—the very people who stepped in to raise me in their absence.

I forgave this parent and their spouse in my heart—for this and other things that have occurred during the times we were reconnected. The only thing that grieves me now is thinking about all the opportunities I *too* have missed when it came to loving others well.

Unfortunately, the situation with my *other* biological parent (and their side of the family) still stings. And that pain seems to resurface more often these days as all of my kids grow older. Simply put, I wish things were different—that they knew and loved my kids and showed a genuine interest in their lives. While I understand that there are other issues and factors at play that should help me not to take things personally, it doesn't always make it easier. At the same time, due to those "other factors," I'm also aware that it could be God's loving protection and guidance that keeps certain doors closed and even leads us at times to close open ones.

On the bright side, I'm immensely grateful for the family God has blessed me with through my adoption—people who love and accept me and my family unconditionally, just as we are. Their steadfast support and inclusive nature, treating us as if we were their own flesh and blood, mean more than words can express. From our immediate and extended relatives to our friends who've become like family long ago (such as our 'Aunt' Lynnie), we love and appreciate you all so very much.

Knowing that we would struggle, Jesus set the perfect example of how to welcome, heal, and love those who were rejected and outcast. It must have been incredibly liberating to not only be accepted, but to be openly and unashamedly validated by the one and only Messiah. This same Messiah is with you and I today.

Maybe you have a string of deeply painful rejections that all hurt the same, or maybe there's one big moment that still stings. Either way, know that Jesus is eager to embrace you too. When the world crosses its arms and looks away, His arms are always wide open, and He's looking straight into *your* eyes!

Write down the times you've felt rejected.

_____

_____

_____

_____

_____

What other emotions did you experience?

_____

_____

_____

_____

_____

Can you recall any times in which you may have caused _others_ to feel rejected, whether intentionally or unknowingly?

_____

_____

_____

Do you ever feel led by the Lord to seek their forgiveness?

_____

_____

_____

_____

_____

In Psalm 27:10, David writes,

"For my father and my mother have forsaken me, but the Lord will take me in."

His parents didn't literally forsake him, but in essence, he is saying even if they did, He knows God would still be with him. How do his words impact you on a personal level?

_____
_____
_____
_____
_____

What thoughts come to mind when you consider how Jesus was rejected, and often still is?

_____
_____
_____
_____
_____
_____
_____
_____
_____
_____
_____

TWO

Fishers of Men

The bright fluorescent lights, tall black stools, and long industrial-style tables are still fresh in my mind. During this particular semester of art school, Thursday evenings meant Theory and Development of Form. *Theory and Development of Form* ... the class filled with wonderfully unique and creative artists who jumped at any opportunity to think outside of the box. It was the class that changed my life forever.

"Pssst ... There's something weird about our teacher. It's like ... he's glowing," I whispered to my new friend—a dedicated wife, sweet mama, and fellow artist who was much more mature than I was. Juggling her family, school, and job in the way she did was admirable. She was a blonde superhero with a book-bag, and she had the best laugh anyone could ever hear. It could awaken someone from their grave just to laugh with her.

"I think he's … a Christian," she whispered back hesitantly.

Our instructor was an interesting man, and his long, unruly brown hair went with the wild look in his eyes—like peanut butter goes with jelly. Yet, there also seemed to be this gentleness and uncontainable passion inside of him that would often bubble up and pour into our classroom. Furthermore, there was something striking and otherworldly about his designs that I couldn't quite put my finger on. The authenticity that seemed to be behind his gentleness drew me in like a gravitational pull. *What is it about this man that feels so safe, and why is it such a big deal?* Questions swirled through my mind rapidly. I couldn't let it go anymore, so I decided to demand an explanation via email. Once the class was over for good, that's exactly what I did, and we eventually exchanged phone numbers. Texting wasn't as common as it is today, but I'll never forget the words that eventually popped up on my screen soon after we began chatting…

"I'm a warrior for Jesus Christ," he texted.

I've heard the name of Jesus and always knew in my heart He was real. There was even a part of me that always loved Him, oddly enough. I was never fully committed to Him, but this time, seeing His name in that message humbled me to the point of sitting down on the nearby steps. I've just been hit in the chest, unexpectedly, with a ton of spiritual bricks! Questions and thoughts flooded my mind even more than they had before… *What does this mean for me? What does this mean for my son? Jesus truly is real, and He's the reason why this man is so different!* My heart might as well have melted into a puddle right there on the floor. I'd actually *seen* Jesus inside of someone else.

Then, this teacher did the unthinkable ... he invited me to *church.*

Panicked about what to wear, I went shopping for something "churchy." I settled on a pair of black dress pants, a black shirt, and of course, a black pea coat. I figured everyone needs a peacoat for church ... right? He picked me up that snowy January morning, and off we went into the unknown.

Prior to the sermon, the pastor recommended the congregation pray out loud. Between listening to this room full of strangers' voices and seeing their hands up in the air for no reason, my face grew hot. I was very uncomfortable, but I also knew that if I could run, I wouldn't.

When he dropped me off after service, I walked straight upstairs to my bedroom and prayed on my knees. It was like lightning hit my veins, and my understanding began to open. Something in me knew I was *home,* and that all the insatiable hunger I had for the supernatural would finally be satisfied in Jesus. All of a sudden, I knew why this satisfaction couldn't be found in the things I've tried before as a kid—like playing the ouija board or playing "light as a feather, stiff as a board" with friends during sleepovers. There was no hope in either of those boards! It also wasn't in the mediums I sought out to reconnect with my son's late father or in the dreams I had that always seemed to foretell the future.

Soon after this experience, I dreamt of snow falling on my face as I slowly spun in circles, eyes upward, looking into the vast white sky. Each snowflake not only felt like it was filled with God's love, it felt like it *was* God's love. In an interview about his testimony, I heard music artist and online personality, Big Nik, say that as he learned about Jesus, he felt like his eyes turned into hearts, similar to a cartoon character or the heart-eyes emoji. That's the only way I can describe what this time was like for me too. It felt like Jesus was with me everywhere! The sunshine felt different, the rain felt different, and the world around me even looked different. My body was the same, but I was different.

My Christian journey was by no means perfect after this point. In fact, we don't have nearly enough time nor space to discuss every wrong turn and bad decision I've made as a believer. It grieves my heart thinking about all the things I've done and said that hurt God and still do at times! However, His power is made perfect in my weakness (2 Corinthians 12:9). I seek to do better each day, even when I fail.

I share all this to say: seeing Christ inside of you can change someone's entire life. Sure, it may sound cliché, but I'm living proof! Do you think my instructor knew when he walked into class that first day that his conduct would result in the salvation of one of his students? I get to spend eternity in Heaven because this art instructor was unashamed of sharing the Gospel (Romans 1:16), pointing me to Christ's death and resurrection. Even my friend, the blonde superhero, faithfully planted seeds of truth during our conversations, despite my spiritual blindness and sailor's mouth. She was a Christian herself, which is how she solved the case of the mysterious glow of our teacher. It was no coincidence that she and I met there, and what a blessing that was. We've created some hilarious memories we still laugh about today. Just like our teacher didn't know, she had no clue that a "special mission" awaited her in that Thursday night class. We're not only friends, but *sisters,* and it's all because of her perseverance and patience back in art school. I admire her even more now than I did back then (and her laugh is still one of my favorite things about her as it highlights the awesome personality God gave her).

Friends, please don't underestimate the power of Christ living in you or the effectiveness of the seeds you plant. People may not always listen, but they're definitely always watching.

When you do your part, God will do His.

Ask the Holy Spirit to show you how you can be a better witness for Christ.

Are there some rough edges that need to be smoothed out? Is your tone a little too harsh? Are you snotty when the church presents new ideas or even when new people show up? Do you doubt you could ever make a difference? Maybe you think some people are "too far gone," and there's no hope for their salvation.

_____

_____

_____

_____

Whatever the issues may be, ask God to help you be more open to the ways He desires to use you. This lost and hurting world needs your willingness to share the best news they'll ever hear—even if they don't receive it. Despite how many people view us Christians and our motives, sharing the Gospel is ultimately a labor of love towards those we are sharing with. After all, eternity is real and "Hell is too long to be wrong" as one of my son's favorite Youtubers, Mapalo, says.

May we all live by the following verse, just as my art instructor did ...

"But in your hearts revere Christ as Lord. Always be prepared to give an answer to everyone who asks you to give the reason for the hope that you have. But do this with gentleness and respect." (Peter 3:15)

THREE

Whistleblower

One of my closest friends, whom I love and respect for more reasons than I can count, recently shared something that keeps coming back to me.

"It seems like everywhere God places me, He calls me to be a whistleblower," shot out of her mouth in pure frustration and despair.

The Lord has placed her in many places where she was challenged to speak up when all she wanted to do was run the other way like Jonah. Yet, she constantly and courageously chose obedience over fear. In the end, God always came through and defended her as she spoke truthful, yet uncomfortable, words. Not only have I been encouraged during the times I've personally witnessed God's faithful defense of her obedience, but it's strengthened my own faith too.

Regardless of the Lord's track record, it's still difficult for her every time He calls her to pick that whistle up again.

Months after she vented to me, I realized it's also the story of *my* life; maybe it's yours too. Due to my sometimes-perceived bluntness, many people might believe I'm very confident, overly bold, or maybe even uncaring. But that couldn't be further from the truth. Choosing to speak up, despite how it may seem on the surface, causes a huge battle in my mind. In fact, it's a greater battle than anyone could possibly imagine—*believe me*. Even in addressing small issues with others that concern me, or my loved ones, the mental war is intense. I often have to remind myself that it's *okay* to voice my needs or concerns, and sometimes the needs and concerns of others (especially if they're vulnerable or helpless). I need God's help, and my heart *always* aches for Him to use what I say to help bring a mutual solution that gives Him glory.

The mental battle I face beforehand is often due to my own insecurities and traumatic life experiences—of which I have many. God knows that speaking up has been a part of my healing journey after some very difficult seasons. Satan has a field day in my mind as he aims to shut me up and tell me I'm crazy. He plants seeds of doubt concerning reality, just like he did to Eve in the garden. Truth be told, he wants to shut *all* of us believers up. He knows all too well that when we obey those scary promptings from our Father, an opportunity for change is created. I believe that's a very powerful thing in the spirit realm.

Even if those on the receiving end of our words don't listen or take heed to how God might be using us, He can still do so much because of our obedience. We won't always see the fruit right away—and sometimes, not at all—but that's okay! In fact, the friend I mentioned earlier had some serious seasons of waiting after God called her to sound the alarm. But when He showed up, He *really* showed up. Unfortunately, we've become so accustomed to staying quiet and avoiding conflict that we end up looking at others who do raise awareness to problems as if *they're* the problem. We've dropped the standard simply because we don't know any better and our emotional intelligence levels have decreased over time. Yours has. Mine has. No one is an exception.

In my opinion (I'm sure an unpopular one), healthy communication training should be mandatory in all companies, organizations, schools, and *especially* in churches! Understanding the importance of speaking up and practicing good listening skills could change the world. Not only would it aid in each other's healing as a society, but it would prevent an abundance of other potential problems.

After all, God calls us to be truth seekers and truth speakers. Yes, there's a time and place for speaking (I'll be the first to admit that I'm not the greatest with timing. It's an ongoing learning process for me). Nevertheless, Ecclesiastes, one of my favorite books of the Bible, doesn't only say there's a time to be *silent* but it also says there's a time to *speak* (Ecclesiastes 3:7). We always talk about the damage speaking up in certain situations can do, but *not* speaking the truth can do just as much damage if not more. Speaking up and sharing feelings should be meant to give others the opportunity to validate those feelings (even if they don't agree or understand), apologize if necessary, and work through the issue together for a common solution. This leaves both parties strengthened and encouraged as edification takes place. If both people's hearts are selflessly seeking unity and truly willing to listen to one another, it can move mountains! I've seen it! The Lord gets the glory, and He shines as restoration and healing takes place.

Furthermore, speaking up for injustices is straight from the Father's heart. Whether it's injustice toward yourself or others, being passive is not in our spiritual DNA. That's why, when someone sees or hears something disturbing but lets it go, it haunts them. We simply weren't wired like that. Christ taught the exact opposite! All of the major, positive events that took place throughout history (including many biblical events), all started with one or more people speaking up. When God uses a willing vessel, things shift in the spirit realm. Not to mention, exposure to the truth should always be the catalyst for healthy change and improvement in our hearts, especially for Christians.

We all can do better.

Do you ever feel like the Lord calls you to be a "whistleblower" too?

_____

_____

_____

_____

_____

Does it feel lonely at times?

_____

_____

_____

_____

How can you embrace this call and pray for more understanding concerning how He wants to use you?

_____

_____

_____

_____

Would you consider yourself a good listener? How can you improve your listening skills?

_____

_____

_____

_____

_____

Do you speak *too* much?

Remember Proverbs 29:11 tells us, "a fool vents all of his feelings, but a wise man holds them back." Ask the Lord to guard your mouth and help you practice the beautiful art of silence when necessary.

_____

_____

_____

_____

_____

Do you ever feel that you're too passive or that you don't speak up enough?

_____

_____

_____

_____

_____

How can you bring this before your Heavenly Father and ask for His help?

_____

_____

_____

_____

_____

Pray for the Holy Spirit to reveal any past wounds that may have contributed to your unhealthy amount of silence.

No matter which of those questions you relate to most and no matter if it's your feelings, matters of injustice, or something in between, seek to speak the truth and listen well. Do it wisely and do it *prayerfully* and be willing to follow your Father's lead without reservations—despite how uncomfortable it may be. He will never steer you in the wrong direction!

Book recommendation:

One Minute Tips For Confident Communication, by Dr. Mike Bechtle

FOUR

Happy Little Trees

Art is such a big part of our household. My two youngest kids and I thoroughly enjoy watching artists in action on YouTube. Whether the person is painting, drawing, or working on some random unconventional project, we're glued to the screen. I often think of what a blessing it is that these incredible men and women are able to showcase their amazing talent in front of the world through technology. I'm so grateful to be able to watch them exercise the gifts God gave them. After all, those talents and abilities are small reflections of *His* creativity and awesomeness—He's *our* Creator!

Often, I doubt the artists' process as I watch them create. Even though I've previously seen some of their work before, and their awe-inspiring track record *clearly* speaks for itself, I still find myself cringing at each step that doesn't seem to make sense. Oh, and don't get me started on Bob Ross. This man would paint the most beautiful scenery and then boom! Smack dab, in the middle of the painting, he paints a long thick black line for the sake of adding another "happy little tree." Everything in me screams, *No, Bob! Don't do it! You're ruining this beautiful piece! We don't need another happy little tree! It's perfect as it is!* But by the time he's finished, I can't imagine the painting without it.

It's easy to forget that it's only a matter of time before every blank space, splatter, and seemingly "out of place" line will be morphed together in perfect harmony. And then, voilá! The final masterpiece is revealed, proving to skeptical viewers like me that beauty can still emerge, no matter how discouraging some initial stages may look or feel. Every detail, or lack thereof, had (or found) a purpose. If the creator is credible and trustworthy, then beauty is going to emerge regardless of the challenge— simply because of the hands creating it.

If a human artist is concerned with the finished product of their artwork, think about how much more God is concerned with the *finished* product of our lives and character. It's not about how we start, it's how we finish, and the process throughout that's crucial. In other words, when our trust is in Him, then each person and season He paints into our lives— even the happy little accidents—all contribute to the beauty of the final masterpiece. Not only are His hands the most credible and trustworthy of all, but He always has a plan! So, no matter where He decides to place new "happy little trees" in our lives, and no matter how scary it may look at first, let's wisely choose to trust His process. Remember, He's not finished with us yet!

What lessons have you learned from the "happy little accidents" that have occurred in your lifetime?

_____

_____

_____

_____

_____

How can you learn to trust God's process more? (Perhaps reflecting back on times when He added new, unwanted "trees" against your will, can encourage you!)

_____

_____

_____

_____

Read the following verses as well as the surrounding context: Proverbs 3:5, Isaiah 26:3, Romans 8:28, and Philippians 1:6.

What themes and/or patterns do you notice?

_____

_____

_____

_____

_____

_____

_____

_____

FIVE

Such a Time as This

I've been sorting through a lot of my parents' old photos recently. As I traveled through the last five (plus) decades, my emotions alternated between joy and grief. Part of me was having the time of my life because, in my opinion, there's nothing more beautiful than an authentic black-and-white vintage photo. However, the other part of me grieved, not only over the loss of beloved family members who have since passed away, but because of the loss of simpler times. I couldn't stop thinking about how much has changed over the years as I journeyed through each moment, frozen in time. There always seemed to be just enough room on the couch for the abundance of cousins, friends, neighbors, and the neighbors' cousins and friends. Life was lived *together,* plain and simple. It didn't matter if your kid had chicken pox or any other contagious funkiness, send 'em on over because we'd rather all get it than be away from one another!

There was so much freedom in every smile. It was evident they were untouched by technology addictions, fear of daily life, and the pride of their own self-built walls—as many of us are today. I could almost feel the plaid velvet couch on my skin, hear the laughter, and smell the cigarette smoke. It was a time of station wagons, console TVs, and phones that were attached to the wall rather than our hands.

It was certainly different back then, and the past had its own issues of course, but my heart still aches for those times. Nonetheless, no matter how often we resurrect bell-bottoms or watch awesome nostalgic TV shows and movies, we simply can't go back.

On the bright side, my rollercoaster of emotions eventually slowed to an attitude of gratitude. I thought about how grateful I was (and still am) that *God* doesn't change. He's not sitting in Heaven waiting for the next fashion trend, and He's surely not changing His Word or personal views like we change our shoes. Nothing about Him changes, ever. He's the same yesterday, today, and forever (Hebrews 13:8). How comforting it is to know that togetherness and community, the way it was intended to be, will still happen one day in a place where it can't be contaminated by the toxicity of our own selfishness. Everything will be made right, and it will *stay* right for all of eternity— peace and rest, at last.

Does your heart also get heavy when you think about the good old times and the current state of the world? If so, remember nothing surprises God. This life here on Earth is temporary, and you were created for such a time as this. You have a very specific part to play in the Great Commission before it's time to go home. We have to take a deep breath, stand tall, listen earnestly to His voice, and then do our best to fulfill that purpose well, while there's still time left.

How can you play a part, personally, in bringing back old traditions in order to bless others? Even if it's as simple as welcoming a new neighbor with a homemade pie, it counts!

_____

_____

_____

_____

_____

Ecclesiastes 7:10 reads,

"Do not say, 'Why were the old days better than these?' For it is not wise to ask such questions."

What are your thoughts on this passage?

_____

_____

_____

_____

_____

Read the surrounding text and pray for deeper insights.

Do you think looking back can sometimes rob us of gratitude, contentment, and possibilities for the present and future? Why or why not?

_____

_____

_____

_____

_____

SIX

A Turned Ship

Counseling, marriage conferences, private seminars, books, articles, videos ... nothing worked. Our marriage was toxic and abusive. I was a mess. He was a mess. Something was seriously wrong. No one else seemed to struggle as badly as we did. I often wondered, why was *our* marriage like this?

Finally ... I did it.

Ten years and two more kids later ... I moved out with practically nothing and started life over.

Don't get me wrong. Despite our personal issues, we've always maintained a friendship within our marriage. We often shared our thoughts and experiences, chatted on the phone throughout the workday, and ultimately bonded over our similar senses of humor and love for Jesus. Even while we lived apart, my husband remained a faithful father to our kids, staying active in their lives.

However, for lack of better words, there was still this sinister black cloud we couldn't seem to shake. The cloud brought confusion and damage to us and to those around us (especially to those who attempted to help us but truly didn't understand the extreme depths of the spiritual warfare we were dealing with). Then, there were others who "tried" to help us but inflicted even more pain and suffering into our already fragile union. Sadly, these leaders were used by Satan right under our noses, and we didn't even see it.

During this season, I knew I had to drown out the many voices (and opinions) around me in order to hear my Redeemer's voice. I stained my new and unfamiliar floor with many tears and worshiped my aching heart out. God held my hand and protected me fiercely under His mighty wing, even during the times I wanted to leave His security and run away. Where to? I wasn't exactly sure. I felt His supernatural strength and loving, Fatherly protection in a way I never had before. No one was messing with His girl.

Once our divorce papers were filed and ready, I consulted the Heavens with no particular plan or request. I just knew I needed to look up even more intently than before; the pain of reality was unbearable. I wasn't necessarily seeking His help to "save" the marriage, because my husband and I were both on board with the divorce. But a crazy, and very unexpected, shift occurred. The ship started to turn. We found ourselves willing to try again, despite all odds, yet with no clue of just how much God would be on our side.

There were so many ups and downs during this attempted reconciliation. We were back in the boat, but the waters were anything but calm. It was going to be a wild journey, and I often wondered if it was one I should even take. I'm sure my husband felt the same way. During those first few months, in His beautiful sovereignty, God brought a friend into my life (who is now a very close sister). It all started with her encouraging me to read a book titled, *Discovering the Mind of a Woman,* by Ken Nair. Initially, I declined as the title was clearly for men—and it sounded boring. I also figured it would be a waste of time—or worse—it would leave me feeling even more discouraged.

But she convinced me.

As I read the very surprising words, page after page, tears of joy silently rolled down my cheeks. Overall, they were a mixture of relief, freedom, and gratitude. Relief that I wasn't crazy in things that I've sensed and discerned throughout my life as a woman. Freedom from the burden of lies and unrealistic expectations put on my gender by society (and even by the church). And lastly, gratitude—not only for the Lord's specific design for men and women as individuals—but for the fact that He brought a resource into my hands that actually made sense! It lined up with His Word more than anything else we've come across in those previous 10 years, and believe me, we've come across a lot. One of the many pictures it humbly painted was that God loves and defends women *so, so, so* much more than we realize, even as devout Christians. Sure, this seems to be a given that all believers would already know, but many of us haven't even scratched the surface. I learned that all the abuse that's happened in our marriage hurt God even more than it hurt me.

My husband read the book as well and was immediately impacted. As its concepts began to sink in, his heart began to scratch the surface of what true, biblical masculinity means (as well as the depths of responsibility that come along with it). There were often times when he couldn't even finish a sentence without crying. His heart began softening right before my eyes, and it was actually genuine!

Thankfully, God led us down a path of getting the *right* kind of help … long-term, biblically-based, healthy, and "safe" help. This ongoing support has brought (and is still bringing) us to a place of maturity in our marriage that was obviously much needed.

Now, we are experiencing what a healthy marriage looks like, and it's been such a blessing as we love and understand each other so differently now. In fact, we often joke about what it's like getting to know each other all over again, as "new people." I'm even grateful for the simple things, such as laughing together so often. Furthermore, seeing the way it's impacted our children has been one of the biggest blessings of all. Of course we aren't perfect, and never will be, but we are in a really good place now and have so much more peace than we've ever had in our marriage.

Learning all these (and more) concepts, at such a deeper level spoke volumes to my broken and weary heart. The gray cloud began to dissipate, and I was left falling deeper in love with Jesus. On the contrary, I was also left broken, thinking about the grief God must feel over hearing the cries of so many women who truly don't understand His heart toward them. This is especially true for women who've endured trauma in their marriage like I have. Sadly, most women don't know what it feels like to be loved, protected, and defended by a man—not in the way God intends, anyway.

Countless husbands and fathers are dropping the ball simply because no one's ever taught them how to hold it. Then, us women see the ball sitting there and attempt to pick it up ourselves outside of God's perfectly designed plan, further escalating the issue. Our world is clearly feeling, manifesting, and sometimes even celebrating, the effects of this calamitous, spiritual tragedy. Destructive learned behaviors and toxic patterns will always continue on into each new generation until we deal with it spiritually.

Although Nair's focus in the book and personal discipleship programs is on holding men accountable to Christlikeness, it by *no means* excuses women from our sins. We will still have to give an account for our lives and decisions one day too. In fact, it's crucial we keep our hearts in check because God gave wives the honorable role of the Hebrew term, Ezer Kenegdo, meaning "helpmeet." Ezer means "to rescue/save" (or to be strong), and Kenegdo means "opposite to." In other words, we are meant to be a humble alarm for our husbands when they get off track with the Father and to oppose their rebellion toward Him. More often than not, the honest mental state and feelings of a wife reveal to her husband (and sometimes to the world) how he's doing with the Lord. He has to pay close attention and be open to hearing the truth of the issues without immediately defending himself, in the flesh. He must understand and honor the fact that she's a gift (Proverbs 18:22), and that if he humbles himself and values her feelings and opinions, even when they're difficult to hear, it will be of *great* benefit to him. Although it's not our only purpose, God knew that men would need some help keeping their eyes on Him.

In her wonderfully enlightening book, *I'm Finally Free To Be Me,* Nancy Nair (Ken Nair's wife) states,

> "A woman needs to be able to always speak the truth, because God has required her to do that as his helpmeet. Holding it in will bring damage to her spirit. The goal is to help a husband with his un-Christlike attitudes, such as the emotion of anger."

In order to do this job (and any other jobs the Lord has for us), we need to stay close to our Heavenly Father and continuously deal with the wickedness of *our* own hearts. I've spent so many years living in frustration because I didn't know the grave importance of being led by the Holy Spirit in my marriage—especially when it came to my tongue. Couple that with a past full of hurt, and you have a recipe for disaster. I've learned a lot and still have quite a long way to go, but I think it's safe to say it's going to take a lifetime!

Nonetheless, living in the grace of a restored marriage is

extremely humbling. It serves as a constant reminder of how I was, and still am, in desperate need of God every moment of every day. I ... *we* learned the hard way that we simply can't afford to have anyone other than Him steering our ship, and what a merciful Captain He is.

Is God the captain of *your* "ship" (whatever that may be)? Have you willingly given Him full permission and control over your life and circumstances … prepared for any and all outcomes?

_____

_____

_____

_____

_____

Do you find it easy or difficult turning to God during challenging times?

_____

_____

_____

_____

_____

When in your life has God made the impossible, possible? In what ways has seeing Him work humbled you?

_____

_____

_____

_____

_____

What lies have you been told and believed concerning marriage and/or gender roles?

_____

_____

_____

_____

*If you're currently being abused whether physically, mentally or both, please seek help *immediately*. Let people in and accept the support, but use extreme caution concerning who you trust.

If possible, create physical distance between you and your spouse so you can live under separate roofs as you begin healing and growing. Please prioritize your safety during and even after this process.

For help, call the National Domestic Violence Hotline at **(800) 799-7233**.

Lastly, chase your Heavenly Father with all your heart, and take things one day at a time. He's the only one who knows what's best for *your* specific circumstance as all of our situations are different.

*Highly recommended books concerning marital abuse and setting boundaries:

The Emotionally Destructive Marriage, by Leslie Vernick

Boundaries in Marriage, by Henry Cloud and John Townsend

Codependent No More, by Melody Beattie

*Highly recommended books concerning marriage and understanding the truth about biblical gender roles:

Discovering the Mind of a Woman, by Ken Nair

Discovering the Heart of a Man, by Ken Nair

I'm Finally Free To Be Me, by Nancy Nair

SEVEN

I Saw Angels!

"Me and my friends saw demons at the park, and someone told the teacher. The demons had a boss and there was scary music playing."

These were the first words out of my then-six-year-old daughter's mouth when I picked her up after school. It's certainly not what any parent expects to hear when they ask their child how their day was. I listened to more details in the following two minutes it took to get home. After we parked, I asked if the experience scared her, to which she replied, "No because I know Jesus was with us, and He's bigger."

Once we walked in the door (both of us still processing), she headed straight for the paper and crayons.

"What are you doing, baby?" I asked.

"I'm drawing them," she replied. As she colored rapidly,

laser-focused on showing me what they looked like, it felt like I had suddenly entered into a scene of a scary movie. At that time, I didn't know as much about demons and the supernatural. I'm still learning, and always will be, but it was a foreign concept then—even as a Christian. To think, they saw them in broad *daylight*! I was still completely stunned, of course, but I could tell that this experience was real in my baby girl's eyes, and that's what mattered.

Unsure of what else to do, I decided to check in with her teacher, who confirmed that another student did in fact approach her with the same claims. The class was visiting the local park because the school playground was under construction at the time. The teacher said she just assumed they were using their imaginations in the change of scenery. In an attempt to find a tangible explanation (and make sure my daughter was really okay after this experience), I took her back to the playground. When I asked her to show me where this happened, she pointed to the nearby backyard of a house that appeared to be vacant. I'm not going to lie, it was a little eerie, but again, I wasn't sure *what* to think. Interestingly, during this time, there were a lot of very strange things happening in our lives and even in our home. Looking back, I know, without a shadow of doubt, that our family was under an intense spiritual attack.

As I began to learn more about the supernatural in the time following this incident, I slowly started teaching my youngest kids too. We read scripture more often and enhanced our prayers when it came to fighting in the spirit. Honestly, they seemed to understand it so well; it was as effortless to them as breathing air. Again, I had been a believer for many years at this point, yet still had a hard time wrapping my head around the fact that spiritual warfare is right under our noses, daily.

Even though the Gospel is supernatural in and of *itself*, so many of us Christians still miss the big picture when it comes to the concept of good and evil. On the other hand, many kids understand things that pertain to magic. After all, TV shows, movies, toys, and clothing are all flooded with yin-yang symbols, all-seeing eyes, wizards, and everything in between. Sadly, the occult has been glorified, normalized, and presented as innocent, positive, or mere "fantasy." Even the *Ouija board* blends in on store shelves as if it's just another option for family game night! Popcorn and summoning demons, anyone?

Children are pure in heart and can very well see things adults don't. In fact, when my youngest son was a toddler—long before my daughter's experience—he heard me mention the word "angels" when I was talking on the phone. In his sweet little voice, he excitedly said, "I saw angels!"

Intrigued, I asked, "You saw angels?"

Quickly pointing upward at the ceiling, he exclaimed, "Yeah, they took me up to God! They had big wings and were *really* blurry!"

Startled, I asked another question. "What did God look like, bud?"

Visibly frustrated and shaking his head from side to side, he replied, "He was too bright!" He was also squinting his eyes as if a bright light was shining directly in his face.

I gave it a few minutes and asked again. He repeated the

same thing but decided to stomp out of the room as if he had had enough of my ridiculous questioning. I never taught him about angels, and I was caught completely off guard by what he said and how upset he was as he said God was simply "too bright." It was evident he was sad that he couldn't get a good look at Him, but at the same time thinking, *why aren't you getting it, Mom! What's so hard to understand about me seeing angels?* It was clear he was recalling a very real experience, just like his sister's account that came years later.

Many years after this conversation with my youngest son, I read *Visions of Heaven and Hell,* by John Bunyan. As Bunyan recalls a personal Heavenly experience, he states, "God was too bright for me to look upon as He was exalted on the high throne of His glory, while multitudes of angels and saints sang forth eternal hallelujahs and praises to Him." Furthermore, 1 Timothy 6:16 says, "who alone is immortal and who lives in unapproachable light, whom no one has seen or can see. To him be honor and might forever. Amen." My, oh my—what a sight that must be! It's neat knowing my baby got an early glimpse of that glorious light.

Surely it's a sad time we're living in, as the Devil works overtime to rip the faith, hope, and innocence right from under our little ones. He zealously uses whatever and whomever he can ... cultural messages, peers, teachers, leaders, social media, and even a child's own parents to influence them toward the wrong paths. The absolute worst thing we can do is ignore him and keep our heads in the clouds because darkness makes us uncomfortable (or because we feel we're giving him "undeserved attention"). We should ignore him and his demons just about as much as we'd ignore a burglar coming into our home or a creepy guy lurking around the park. Satan comes to steal, kill, and destroy. Period. To ignore him is absurd and leaves us and our families more vulnerable than ever. We have to fight, and we certainly can't afford to take childrens' spiritual eyes lightly. They are a gift, and there's a tremendous amount we can learn from them and their keen awareness.

I'm not saying we need to see things in the same exact manner as children do, or that we should chase these spiritual experiences. Satan will use even that to ensnare us if we're not careful. However, we do need to be aware and mindful of the spiritual world around us. Seeking to understand and navigate it all in a way that honors God is not only wise, it's biblical.

Furthermore, it's incredibly important that we take our kids seriously when they share their experiences. Sure, there are often natural explanations or heightened imaginations that we can explain to help them process. Regardless of their experiences, we should do our best to listen well, validate their feelings, and pray. We have to teach them how to fight in the spirit for themselves too. Raising up warriors, especially in these times, is an honor and privilege even when it's difficult.

Has a child (whether your own or someone else's) ever shared an experience that made you feel confused or uncomfortable? How did you handle it?

Why do you think children are so sensitive to the spirit realm?

_____

_____

_____

_____

_____

Over time, how is this sensitivity affected by the world around them?

_____

_____

_____

_____

_____

Can you recall any experiences from your own childhood that brought you closer to God or perhaps instilled fear?

_____

_____

_____

_____

_____

_____

_____

_____

_____

_____

_____

EIGHT

Close to Dad

My youngest son is very affectionate. It never surprises me when he hugs me out of nowhere. Whether I'm cooking, reading, or even walking in or out of a room, he unapologetically wraps his arms around me for a quick squeeze. Then, he continues on to his other missions of the day without skipping a beat. I've come to learn that it's *his* way of saying "I love and appreciate you, Mom" and it makes my heart smile every single time.

But his affection doesn't just extend to me. After God reconciled my husband's and my marriage just before our divorce was finalized (as you've read in a previous entry), our son became even more affectionate toward him. To this day, he unapologetically climbs all over him, sits on lap, messes with his beard and is simply enamored with him. I'm sure to some, it might look and seem odd (understandably so) because he's a big kid! Despite the fact that he's a typical "boy's boy," he doesn't shy away from his own tenderness because, well, he *missed* his Dad. You see, although my husband was still involved in our kids' lives during our separation, he became a different man then ... and our son knew it. My husband wasn't living the greatest life (which he openly admits himself and doesn't mind me sharing), but our son and daughter still didn't give up hope and continued to pray for him. We later found out that if it weren't for those prayers, at the specific times that they prayed, life would have turned out very differently to say the least.

When we got back together, they were a few years younger then and could hardly contain their excitement. In fact, the first time we had a family outing again, it was silliness, giggles, and squealing galore.

My husband doesn't mind the extra affection from my son. He always says, "They're going to be adults too, in the blink of an eye." Not that *that* would stop us from loving on them ... we still hug our first borns too. As crazy as our household was at times, my husband especially never shied away from being affectionate toward our oldest son—not even during the scary teenage years.

After God lovingly led my husband back to Him, my husband showed our son a picture I took. Our son added "my Daddy" to a prayer wall at a church we were visiting, and I'm so glad I felt compelled to capture that moment. As they sat in those church chairs and stared at the photo, my husband told him, "Thank you for praying for me, buddy. Your prayers are why I'm here right now." They hugged and cried together.

Our boy remembers what life was like when he wasn't as close to his Dad. His little, yet so very big, heart knows that every moment is a gift and reminder that our family is living out an answered prayer. He's not looking around to see if his friends are climbing on their dads or paying any mind to anything else. He happily welcomes the safety and security of his father's strong arms. He always wants to be where he is, and he basks in every moment with him ... fishing, hunting, playing around and simply talking about life. A little boy and his dad ...

Now, a few years later while at church, my inner, strict mama sought to come out. I wanted my son to sit away from his dad so he could focus and pay attention better. *Oh, here we go again, he's too big for this,* I thought. But this time, the Lord impressed on my heart that it's a beautiful thing and that it's the type of relationship He desires to have with *His* own children too. He wants us to snuggle up close to Him and doesn't want anyone deterring us just like Jesus didn't want his followers stopping the children from sitting with Him.

Friend, you and I are more than welcome to sit on the Father's lap too, no matter what others around us say or do in an attempt to stop us. I'm reminded of John's posture during the moment Jesus told his disciples that one of them would betray Him.

Let's read it together...

"When Jesus had thus said, he was troubled in spirit, and testified, and said, Verily, verily, I say unto you, that one of you shall betray me. Then the disciples looked one on another, doubting of whom he spake. Now there was leaning on Jesus' bosom one of his disciples, whom Jesus loved. Simon Peter therefore beckoned to him, that he should ask who it should be of whom he spake. He then lying on Jesus' breast saith unto him, Lord, who is it?" (John 13:21-25 KJV)

The King James version makes it clear that the disciple "whom Jesus loved" (widely believed to be John), didn't shy away from wanting to be close to Jesus. In fact, back in those days, it was perfectly normal for men to be affectionate with one another as part of their culture. It was a beautiful thing, just as the affection between a father and son is today. Just recently, one of my relatives said it saddens her that "my husband and another family member of hers are the only two men she's ever witnessed loving on their boys."

Society desperately needs more strong men who aren't ashamed to love and be loved. But this starts with them (and all of us) first climbing onto our Abba's lap, studying every feature, and simply being thankful to be there. After all, there were times when we were separated from Him too.

Sure, others may not always understand why we want to be so close to our Daddy, and that's okay. They don't know what we've been through …

Growing up, was your dad affectionate toward you?

_____

_____

_____

_____

_____

How did this affection, or lack thereof, make you feel?

_____

_____

_____

_____

_____

How do you think a strong father-son relationship impacts a child's emotional well-being and development?

_____

_____

_____

_____

Why do you think so many men are hesitant to show tenderness and vulnerability toward their children or even toward one another?

_____

_____

_____

_____

_____

_____

_____

_____

_____

_____

NINE

The Right Way Really Is Better

I had to play mediator in a debate between my kids and our neighbors–two brothers they've become good friends with. The issue was centered around the correct way to play the boardgame, *Sorry.* The boys explained the rules and how my kids have been playing incorrectly (which I take full responsibility for because I'm lazy when it comes to board game instructions). I explained to my frustrated daughter that we were wrong and should try their way instead because it makes more sense. "Do we have to? That way will be boring ... the wrong way is more fun!" she whined.

I smiled at the hidden spiritual nugget and explained how I dropped the ball by not reading through the rules thoroughly enough. Then I let her know how grateful we should be that they're teaching us a new and better way. They ended up having a good old time filling the house with the sound of giggles and minor disagreements over who moved too many spaces.

So many of us have assumed God's way is boring, too. I certainly have had those thoughts during some of my darkest seasons of suffering. While sharing her testimony with me, one of my old childhood friends said, "I always held back from coming to God. I thought if I fully surrendered to Him my life would be boring, but when I did get saved, that's when the adventure started." God has done so many things she's never imagined in her life, including giving her a job where she gets to meet celebrities on a regular basis. When we open ourselves up to God, the possibilities are endless. It doesn't always look like worldly success or the life my old friend lives, but spiritual success is an absolute guarantee in walking consistently with Him. We can't go wrong when we ask Him to direct the life that *He* gave us in the first place.

Following the Bible spares us from additional and unnecessary heartache. Life is hard enough *with* the Bible let alone *without* it. Why would we not take that additional, and ultimately, *eternal* help? This game of life is so much better and more exhilarating when we pay closer attention to our instruction manual. I've heard it said that an acronym for Bible is "**B**asic **I**nstructions **B**efore **L**eaving **E**arth." In my opinion, the church doesn't teach enough about how to follow the Bible correctly. It's become acceptable to skip over and even rewrite some of the most vital commandments, which in turn changes the entire "game." It's no wonder everything is out of whack in the world, and it will only get worse as scripture tells us. Society has practically thrown the instructions in a giant bonfire and ignorantly danced around it as it burned. But burning, mocking, attempting to change, or simply *neglecting* the Word of God does not take away its truth, power, or final authority.

And unlike a perfectly square board game, life is more like a labyrinth. Only the Lord provides the type of fun and joy that satisfies the human heart–in a way no person or thing ever could. His rules are perfect by default because only He knows where each path leads or doesn't lead.

Let's choose to play His way instead.

Are you ever tempted to think the Christian lifestyle is (or would be) boring?

_____

_____

_____

_____

Are you reluctant when it comes to others showing you new and better ways to do certain things? If so, do you remember always being this way or did it start at a certain point in your life? Pray for deeper revelation.

_____

_____

_____

_____

_____

Do you ever struggle with following rules or with the idea of others exercising authority over you? If so, where do you think that comes from?

_____

_____

_____

_____

TEN

Giftings and Glory

I'll never forget the moment in 11th grade when I sat at my desk, feeling bewildered. I had recently turned in a paper written about the allegory, *The Wizard of Oz*. It was great that I had gotten an A, but I didn't understand *how*. Although I was very grade conscious since I was a teen mom now, I'd written it quickly and was preparing to accept a C. My true concern was making sure it was written neatly enough.

After high school, I majored in interior design at the Art Institute of Pittsburgh. In one class, the assignment was to create a design and to write a paper about a pre-existing design (using any public place). Once my work was graded, I was left disappointed. My instructor practically ignored my hard work on the design but gave me an A on the essay portion. He announced to the class that my writing was the standard they were to follow. Any inkling that I had a gift for writing went right over my head, because I felt inadequate at that moment. Did I belong in art school at all? I *loved* design, and the need to "create and transform" ran through my veins and still does. However, it seemed as if I only thrived when it came to words. In my mind, there was truly nothing special about my written work.

Not long after this, my English instructor offered me a job as a tutor in our school's writers' center. My very first job was being paid to help other students with their writing assignments, and I *still* didn't get it.

My heart simply wasn't there, and my mind wasn't either, which is odd when I think about it. Since childhood, I've always processed my feelings through writing. If I misbehaved, which was often, or had some other type of issue, I'd write my feelings to my mom and slip them under her bedroom door. She'd eventually see it and write back. That's how we'd share our hearts. It was sweet … her willingness to enter my world and meet me where I was. (I'm still a mama's girl to this day—love you, Mom!)

On top of that, when my son's dad died during my pregnancy, I felt like I *had* to write, and what I wrote became my first book. Clearly, I never saw writing as a "gift" or even saw myself as an author (to be honest, it sounds weird even now when I hear myself referred to as an author). Writing was just something that felt easy. When emotions were high, it felt crucial. It was and still is, therapy for my soul, especially when I'm able to glorify God in this way.

Little did I realize, gifts usually do come effortlessly. Sure, they take work, and your skills sharpen over time with experience, but if it's in you, *it's in you.* Now, I can see it's something my Heavenly Father saw fit to build into my spiritual DNA even before my birth. I'm not the best writer, of course, and that's okay. There's always going to be someone better than us when it comes to our various gifts and talents, but that doesn't mean we shy away from using them. If I compared myself to the wonderful, late legend, C.S. Lewis, I would quit right now—on the spot. My words could never even grace the same paper as his!

As Jon Acuff says in his book, *Soundtracks*, "That's true of any profession. There are better writers than me. That's not false humility; that's a fact." I'd have to say though, Jon is a pretty darn good writer.

I hope you can see your natural talents too! I know for a fact you have them. *Please* don't let them die; they're a part of God's perfect plan for your life. They exist to bring Him glory and to inspire others. Truth be told, the ability to use them for the Kingdom is a great honor that we truly don't deserve. The very act of operating within your gifts, for the sake of God's glory, also brings so much joy to our weary hearts (hence, writing being like therapy for me).

The spiritual gifts listed in Romans 12:6-8 (such as prophecy, teaching, mercy etc.) work in tandem with our talents. These gifts are also wired into our very beings. In fact, Paul had the same gift prior to his conversion. Then upon getting saved, he began to use them for Kingdom purposes only. If you've never taken a spiritual giftings test, I highly recommend it. Knowing which gift you score the highest in, will not only increase your self-awareness, but will enter you into new levels of spiritual maturity. This knowledge will also bring you closer to the Lord and build more excitement concerning His plans for your life. Learning about mine (as well as the downsides to it) has been *incredibly* life changing to say the least.

If you feel that your giftings and talents remain undiscovered, pray for the Lord to help you follow the clues and connect the dots, even as you review the past. After all, if anyone can see the details within how beautifully and uniquely crafted you are, it's your Maker!

Heavenly Father,

Thank You so much for the gifts that You've buried deep within our souls. You are absolutely amazing, and we love You so much for all that You are and all that You do. You're the best gift we could ever ask for. Please help us spot our individual talents and then more importantly, offer them up to You. No matter if it seems small or big in the eyes of the world, or where we fall in comparison to others who share similar gifts, we know You have a plan, and we don't want to miss it. Thank You so much for always hearing our hearts and giving us undeserved opportunities to serve You.

In Jesus' name, amen.

In what ways has God gifted you (that you're aware of)? What comes easily to you?

_____

_____

_____

_____

_____

How do these gifts reflect His character?

_____

_____

_____

_____

How can you use your gifts to bring Him glory and make Him proud?

_____

_____

_____

_____

If you've already taken a spiritual gifts test, what gift did you score highest in and how has this knowledge impacted your life?

_____

_____

_____

_____

_____

_____

_____

_____

_____

_____

ELEVEN

Saved by The Bell

When my kids first started at a new school, that meant they'd be riding the bus each morning–well, a school van. The first morning of school, the van arrived and I could tell right away the driver wasn't the warm and fuzzy type. *Great. This is the first time I'm not driving or walking them, and she seems nasty,* I thought. *Why couldn't she be bubbly? Greeting us with a smile from ear to ear and reciting a Girl Scout pledge, promising to get them to and from school safely every day (said in a perky voice, of course, and followed by a proud salute).* Just teasing … kind of.

We were still getting used to the idea of someone else driving them to school. That year was an extremely difficult one for us, and it brought us even closer together. So, you see, these "little" things mattered more to me than they might to another mom. The last thing I wanted, after the difficult changes we just went through, was to feel any apprehension when trusting a complete stranger with my "babies."

The van driver and I had to work out a minor kink concerning the pickup spot. As pleasantly as I could, I asked if she could park closer to our house (where I was told she would be picking them up). This way, the kids would not have to cross the road and walk down the street, as the van door would still be facing the house when she pulled up. In my mind, it made more sense, was convenient for all of us including her, and it seemed to be the safest option. She agreed. After school that day, I asked the kids how the day went and if their driver was kind. Well, apparently, she didn't have any reservations in mumbling about me in front of them–to say the least. She also exclaimed that I need to be grateful for the adjustment she made.

What now? I won't even tell you all the things that ran through my mama bear head at that moment. Yes, I might have let my thoughts go down the wrong path...

But I *was,* in fact, grateful! I thanked her several times and even told her how much I appreciated it–even though it was technically where she was *supposed* to be getting them according to what I was told. This whole situation almost ruined my day, and I knew I was going to say something about her unprofessional grumbling upon seeing her the following morning. It was a matter of *how* to address it in a kind "enough" way. Something needed to be said, right? Wrong.

The Holy Spirit, in that oh so loving and tender voice, spoke softly to my heart: R*emember... you have control. What you do* *with your emotions, and how this plays out, is completely up to you.* Immediately, I was flooded with memories of other instances in which I learned there was freedom in letting go. Feeling better, I quickly brainstormed some ways I could bless her instead (it was time to kick the Devil in his teeth for getting me all stirred up over something so stupid). My conclusion? Muffins. I love giving people gifts and surprises. We all have our love languages, and this is mine–so it came easy. I already planned on blessing this driver lavishly, especially come Christmastime, but I thought, *why not now and why not muffins! It's time for the big guns!* Yes, I know I'm corny or, as the kids say nowadays, "cringe."

The next morning, I only heard my alarm once at the last minute, even though it was set seven times (yes, I'm a seven-time setter). Even still, I'm usually up much earlier than I need to be so that was strange. The kids were still sleeping, the bus was coming in eight minutes, and I believed my muffin mission was compromised now that I'd have to drive them. Somehow, by the grace of God, I scrambled all their stuff together, threw a bag of frozen zucchini in with one of their lunches due to missing ice packs, and put a baseball cap over my curly afro. We managed to get outside right as she pulled up (and some people say miracles don't happen). Greasy-faced and discombobulated, I groggily extended the muffins, while telling her they were hers. Her harsh lines slowly began to melt as I let her know it was a crazy morning. She thanked me for the muffins and then complimented my daughter's outfit. We shared a small, awkward laugh and off they went.

As I walked into the house, I suddenly realized God wanted the morning to go the way it did for a reason! I wondered, *was I going to slip backwards and add some extra "salt" to those muffins if I had more time to replay the situation in my head before she arrived? If she showed a little attitude, would it have triggered me?* I wasn't sure, but I was too tired to care. I just wanted to give her the sugar-filled peace offering and put that water under the bridge. After all, she's an image-bearer, too, and I don't know her life story or struggles. But what I do know is that God loves her, and I'm called to as well.

Looking back, I'm honestly disturbed and embarrassed by how much it initially bothered me, but I'm also grateful for God's sweet grace, even in these incredibly foolish things. My goodness, I have said and done *much* worse than having a cold attitude and mumbling smart comments under my breath. Was her conduct unprofessional and unnecessary? Maybe. But was it *that* serious to affect me the way it did? Absolutely not! I'm so glad I prayed about it the night before, and God intervened to soothe my silly, troubled soul.

Clearly, the Devil knows just where to target in each of our lives, especially when we're coming out of difficult seasons and our knees are still a little wobbly. I'm so thankful God is our strength and refuge, guiding us through those shaky moments!

Are there any trigger areas in your life in which you find yourself more easily offended and tempted to get out of line? When do you fail to consider the big picture?

Do you often replay certain situations or issues through your mind until there's some resolution?

_____

_____

_____

_____

_____

Is there any recent situation you feel was made worse by your own refusal to stop, think, and pray first?

_____

_____

_____

_____

Lord,

Thank You for holding our hands and exposing the compromised areas of our hearts so we can ultimately become stronger, wiser servants for Your glory and Your glory alone. Help us shut our flesh up when it gets loud and help us to habitually seek Your face, Your Word, and Your will. Remind us of how trustworthy You are to fight our battles, whether miniscule or big. Please help us to grow more sacrificially selfless like our perfect Savior. Thank You for the countless, undeserving second chances and do overs that You so freely give us. Thank You for refining us in the fire... including the fires we're responsible for. You're such a merciful Father and a good, good God, even though we are hot messes and then some!

In Jesus' name,

Amen.

TWELVE

Divine Renovations

When my husband and I blended our families, it certainly wasn't like the Brady Bunch. The only "bunch" we were, was a bunch of hot messes who brought our dirty, trash-filled baggage together and called it home. He came from a background marked by childhood abuse and a near-fatal heroin overdose. My experiences involved being a teen mom seeking love in all the wrong places, along with other personal struggles. While we both came to Christ before meeting each other, there were still *a lot* of unhealed wounds that inevitably led to new challenges.

Naturally, our two oldest children experienced different versions of us than our two youngest children have. While we still loved them with all our hearts during our most immature seasons, they've seen us at our worst. They also both faced their own life challenges outside of the effects of *our* brokenness. And although they're still figuring themselves out (understandably so, at the young ages of 21 and almost 21), they're amazing young adults.

God blessed my beautiful bonus-daughter with a nurturing heart and a profound love for children. She wants to be a kindergarten teacher or behavioral therapist—*be still my heart!* Tender, driven, forgiving, and resilient, she has a contagious zeal for life. Her personality lights up every room she enters, just like her dad's. My son is equally remarkable. He's witty, handsome, funny, discerning, talented, and unapologetic in his convictions. He's also extremely introspective in nature; his wheels always turn in deep thought. I cherish our conversations about life, where we explore everything from dreams to dilemmas, and it's safe to say he gets those never-ending wheels from his mama!

All the "should've, could've, would've" thoughts I've spent too much time dwelling on as a parent quickly fade when I focus on the abundance of positive qualities in them. It shows me that even though my husband and I have a list of things we would change if we could go back in time, God is still sovereign. I see them navigating their paths toward who they are meant to be—no matter what society may dictate about who or what they "should" be ... and no matter how others may try to focus on any of their shortcomings. Nonetheless, this journey is a clear indication that God is actively working in their lives. Their stories are still being written, just as all of ours are and for that, I'm thankful.

And despite our past mistakes as parents, they've still allowed us the opportunity to rebuild on undeserved land. This grace has been a cornerstone of our healing, helping us to forge stronger bonds and move forward with hope.

Time and time again, I've witnessed how God can turn trials into powerful narratives of restoration, growth, and healing. So, no matter what my husband and I have done or *failed* to do, it's incredibly comforting to know that nothing can hinder the Lord's power or His love.

What strategies or practices have helped you and your family heal from past wounds?

_____

_____

_____

_____

_____

In what ways can you be more compassionate toward yourself concerning *your* past mistakes, (whether parental or otherwise)?

_____

_____

_____

_____

_____

How have you fostered forgiveness, both within yourself and among family members?

_____

_____

_____

_____

_____

_____

_____

_____

_____

_____

THIRTEEN

Please Don't Make Me Go

My heart felt like it was going to beat out of my chest as I waited anxiously for a phone call from my daughter's doctor. It was late, and my daughter was sound asleep at that moment. During the last few days, she had experienced lower right-side stomach pain and ran a fever. Although she was still eating, drinking, and acting normally, it was concerning. For the record, she is not a complainer–even when she feels bad. One time, I thought she had a minor belly ache. She insisted she was fine and wanted to run to Subway with me to grab dinner for our family. As the employee began making the sandwiches, she projectile vomited all over the floor (and not that it matters, but there was a police officer ordering his food right next to us). I immediately scooped her up and ran out the door, never to return, leaving her berry-filled pink and purple vomit all over the floor. Don't judge me, it was a bad moment.

When she was only six and broke her arm (which was harder on me at times than it was on her, I think), she handled it like a warrior. In fact, after arriving at the hospital and finally getting settled in her bed, the first thing she said was, "If this happened to Eva, I would switch places with her, so she'd never have to feel this pain." Eva is one of her very best friends. My sweet, but not so "baby" girl, was thinking about how she would want to spare *others* such pain. My mama heart was proud. I had the honor of witnessing the beautiful selflessness in my child during such a terrible experience.

The fact that she was still wincing in pain over her stomach (which seemed to be getting worse right before bed), concerned me. I called the on-call doctor, hoping it was not appendicitis. After returning my call and asking me a series of detailed questions, she suggested I wake her up and immediately take her to Children's Hospital, here in Pittsburgh. I packed a bag as fast as possible, woke her and her brother up, dropped her brother off at my mom's house, and headed straight to the hospital. The whole ride there, she was *begging* me not to take her. Her side was still bothering her, and even though she was the toughest cookie around when she broke her arm, I believe that experience left a bad taste in her mouth toward hospitals. The closer we got, the more she begged and pleaded, and the more my mama heart fought thoughts of turning around and wishing it all away.

As I took notice of the battle in my mind and the growing lump in my throat, the Holy Spirit chimed in with His two cents. Before I knew it, the dynamic of my thoughts had dramatically shifted. *This is how the Father's heart feels when His children beg Him to pull them out of the fire; when they plead for Him to let them stay where it's comfortable or beg to be saved from facing a certain experience any longer. Yet, He does what's needed and what's best for them—just like you must do what's best for your child. Even when it hurts deeply to see them suffer. Love does what's necessary under all circumstances.*

Of course I understood how minor this circumstance was in comparison to the "fires" I've been in, as well as the intense, life-changing battles so many others have faced. Nonetheless, the Holy Spirit knew I needed this sweet truth impressed upon my heart at that very moment. I was also reminded that there's no greater act of "necessary love" than that which took place on Calvary 2,000 years ago. Real love, Godly love, will always do what's necessary.

After two days in the hospital, sleep-deprived, and being told twice that she would need surgery based on her ultrasound, I prayed in desperation with my forehead on her hospital bed. Eventually, we were told that her appendix was just "temporarily inflamed" so we could go home. She would be alright! I had never heard of such a thing! I've always thought appendix-related issues were very black and white (and urgent). This gray area didn't make sense, but *thank You, Jesus.*

Sometimes we, as God's children, sit in the back seat crying and begging Him to turn the car around and go in a different direction. It's so easy to forget that He always has our best interest in mind, which is why reading scripture and praying are so important. I can easily recall many moments that felt like He drove the car straight off a cliff and left me alone, midair. The

Devil tried to convince me that I was completely by myself like
Wile E. Coyote, frozen in time right before plummeting to the
ground. But how many of you know that Wile E. doesn't die,
even when it appears that way? He always makes a comeback
that our child-like minds never seemed to question. Through my
own tears and deeper trust in Him, I emerged stronger than ever
for the next episode. So, until the Lord says otherwise, the series
continues.

Think back to times when the Lord has taken you to "places"
you didn't want to go. How did that experience end? What did
you learn from it and, most importantly, how was He glorified?

_____

_____

_____

_____

_____

_____

_____

_____

_____

_____

_____

_____

_____

_____

_____

_____

_____

FOURTEEN

Black Eye, Oh My!

Covid quarantine was a crazy time, as we all know. Some of us spent it remodeling, others adopted pets, and the rest of us curled up in a ball, binge-watching Netflix to pass the time. Simply put, we hoped to return to a normal world, come the end of our series. I spent Quarantine doing a little bit of "all the above." We remodeled the bathroom, got a puppy, and lazily binged Netflix shows. Despite the terrible circumstances, I did enjoy having my family home and close-by, especially my oldest son, who was a teenager then.

Adjusting to online school gave us the toughest time. It was such an abrupt change for everyone in the world, especially for children. I did my best to keep my little ones occupied with fun-themed movie nights and outdoor adventure hikes on new trails we discovered. I even made a funny video, portraying how they acted during online school (giving them and my Facebook friends a good laugh). The puppy was the joyful cherry on top of this mixed scoop of emotions.

Unfortunately, as he began to grow bigger and stronger, the kids were hurt several times while playing with him. He wouldn't ever hurt anyone on purpose (not even a fly!), but like anything else, God used this puppy to teach me a life lesson.

One day, my youngest son was playing with him on the kitchen floor as my sister and I were chatting at the table. They were playing between the dining chairs and the wall without much space in between the two. Our pup knocked him into the wall, and my son hit his face near the corner of his eye. I put ice on it, hoping to ease the pain. I figured he'd be fine … it was just a minor bump.

Well, it turned into a full-blown black eye, and it seemed to last *forever*. His teachers showed a lot of interest in it during his online classes. I get it. They were doing their job, asking him about it. Maybe they were genuinely curious too, but–my gosh– even the thought of anything other than an accident hurt me to my core. I can't even watch *movies* where kids get hurt, let alone hurt my own kids or allow them to be hurt.

To make matters worse, he'd get quiet and give me an uncomfortable, awkward look whenever they asked about it! Little did they know, he told me he was embarrassed by it and felt even more embarrassed when people brought it up. It was like, *great … I've become the mom everyone thinks went Covid crazy.* After this, when people in passing mentioned his eye, I began feeling the unnecessary desire to give them the entire rundown concerning how it occurred.

Now, here's the good news: Once I was finally ready to lean into the Holy Spirit, I began to feel convicted about caring too much over what people thought (or my perception of their thoughts, anyway).

This brought me closer to the Lord. Yes, my son's black eye. God has a purpose even in the silliest of things because He knows our individual hearts and wants to heal and mature us.

We all care about what people think. If we didn't, we wouldn't be human. How much we care about avoiding criticism is the real concern. When we truly begin to live for an audience of One, these things have a way of shrinking to their proper size. Why? Because holding God's opinion above everyone else's inevitably results in peace and freedom from the weight of others' perceptions.

So, when we feel ourselves being pulled by the opinions of others, let's remember what Paul says in Galatians 1:10 ESV, "For am I now seeking the approval of man, or of God? Or am I trying to please man? If I were still trying to please man, I would not be a servant of Christ."

At the end of the day, God is the only one who matters!

Friend, do you need some help letting go of the weight of other people's opinions? Perhaps you struggle with catastrophizing situations, rather than resting in truth and trusting God. If so, go to your Heavenly Father. He'd be delighted to put things in their proper perspective.

Write out the areas that need to be re-focused on God.

FIFTEEN

Drop The Stone, Karen

Do you remember how upset the Pharisees were over Jesus eating with sinners and tax collectors? In modern terms, we might hear, "He can't be serious right now–does he even know who they are? Is He not aware of what they've done?" or maybe, "Come on! Jesus is eating with *those* fools?" Oh, how I love the fact that He *did* know all about what these people did, and that's exactly *why* He unapologetically showered them with validation. "Those people" are exactly who He came for.

We have modern day pharisees also. Sometimes we lovingly refer to them as "Karens." These aren't just women (or men) who demand to see a manager over silly things or complain about their neighbor's blade of grass touching their property. They also represent the people who are often quick to say things like, "Off with their heads! That guy deserves to burn … that woman needs to be locked up for *life*! I just *cannot* believe they did that ... shame on them ... *so unbelievable!*" The list goes on. They speak so passionately–as if they've never done anything wrong themselves. In other words, Karens (and "Kevins") are the judges of all that is right and wrong in the world, and they always have the perfect solutions. Don't we all act this way at times though (as if we hold more authority and innocence than we actually do)?

I know I sure have.

Listen, I get it. Maybe you *haven't* done the dark and evil things that other folks have done–or anything remotely close. But every one of us is still a flawed sinner with our own ugly messes and issues. After all, there's a spiritual battle happening all around us, every second of every minute of every day. Remember Ephesians 6:12 (NIV), "For our struggle is not against flesh and blood, but against the rulers, against the authorities, against the powers of this dark world and against the spiritual forces of evil in the heavenly realms." When we attempt to fight injustice with quick judgements and shaming reactions, we work with the same rulers of the darkness who convince others to steal, kill, and destroy. It's the same weapon; the world's version of violent justice. Yet, Jesus calls us to compassionate conflict management.

I'm reminded of the woman caught in adultery in John 8. Picture it from the perspective of a Pharisee. You're standing there, feeling excited and rather proud to condemn this woman who was caught red-handed. *What a horrible woman,* you think to yourself. *How dare she commit such an act and break the precious, sacred law!*

It's also time to finally trap this Jesus fellow between a rock and a hard place (no pun intended). Both He and this woman now have no way out–talk about a *win-win* situation! The smooth, hard stone feels so good in your hands ... unbeknownst to you, it's a reflection of your own heart.

Bending down, Jesus quietly writes on the ground as if He were a child playing in His own little world. He stands back up and successfully escapes the trap by declaring, "...let the one who has never sinned throw the first stone" (v.7). As soon as the words leave His mouth, they shoot straight to the core of your heart, like an arrow to its target. Ouch.

It was a heavenly mic drop, and the mic fell so far down, it landed on the floors of Hell. The sound of each stone hitting the ground, one by one, was music to the Father's ears. I picture the face of Jesus beginning to blur as this relieved, vulnerable woman looked at Him through her tear-filled eyes, completely shocked and overwhelmed by this undeserved mercy.

We have all sinned, and we all fall short (Romans 3:23). It doesn't say "some of us" or just the people in prison, or the gossipy women at church, or your boss, or even that one cousin who always ruins family functions. It says *all* of us. So, the next time you're tempted to be a pious Karen, remember that you're in need of just as much mercy, if not *more*, than those around you.

Why do you think Jesus had such a gentle and humble posture during His response to the woman's adultery?

When you have your "Karen moments," do you think it could be connected to the weight of *your* own sin or shame?

_____

_____

_____

_____

_____

_____

_____

_____

_____

_____

_____

_____

_____

_____

_____

_____

_____

_____

_____

_____

_____

_____

_____

SIXTEEN

Titanic

There I was, maybe around 10 or 11 years old, having the best sleepover ever as my friends and I teased and giggled about whose boyfriend Leonardo DiCaprio was. We had just watched the new hit movie, *Titanic*, and despite the depths of horror and tragedy, all we cared about was good old Leo in all of his cuteness and glory.

As I grew older, I developed somewhat of an interest in learning more about that devastating incident that took place on the Atlantic Ocean back in 1912. Fascinatingly, there are so many layers yet to be peeled back, including the conspiracy theory that it may not have even *been* the Titanic that sank, but its sister ship, the *Olympic*. Also, I would have never guessed the co-owner of Macy's, Isidor Straus, and his wife were aboard the ship when it sank.

Although 1912 can often feel as far back as the Garden of

Eden, learning more about this catastrophe always feels fresh to me. Unlike when I was a preteen, picturing myself as Rose in the arms of Leo, I now think about the feelings and emotions of the passengers on that fatal night. Once they had full knowledge that the ship was going down, there was literally nothing they could do to stop it.

Those unfortunate passengers, young, old, rich, and poor, were caught completely off guard by the iceberg and its aftermath. There they were, headed to America on the most majestic and extravagant man-made piece of creation ever to be experienced on the deep blue sea. What an adventure and oh what elegance and class filled its interior! Yet, over 1,500 people had no clue, as they set sail that day that they would be waving goodbye for the very last time. One minute life was good, and the next, they were literally fighting for their lives. Just like that, the "unsinkable" hotel on water was mercilessly swallowed up by the ocean in less than three hours.

While I understand these are two drastically different situations, the suddenness of this tragedy reminds me of Jesus' words in Matthew 24:36-41.

"But about that day or hour no one knows, not even the angels in heaven, nor the Son, but only the Father. As it was in the days of Noah, so it will be at the coming of the Son of Man. For in the days before the flood, people were eating and drinking, marrying, and giving in marriage, up to the day Noah entered the ark; and they knew nothing about what would happen until the flood came and took them all away. That is how it will be at the coming of the Son of Man. Two men will be in the field; one will be taken and the other left. Two women will be grinding with a hand mill; one will be taken and the other left."

No one knows the day or the hour when either Christ returns or our life on earth will end. No matter how cozy, safe, and comfortable the atmosphere may feel at times, we have no control over the inevitable. The only thing we *do* have control over is how we spend our final moments here. Every minute is one step closer to eternity. Today's a good day to decide where you will spend it.

With all that said, let's seek to have a heart like David did in Psalm 90:12. In his insightful declaration to the Lord, He says, "Teach us to number our days so that we may gain a heart of wisdom."

Tomorrow is not promised, beloved.

After the sinking of the Titanic, the passengers' names were put into two categories: *saved* and *lost*. Their money, status, and physical destinations no longer mattered.

Do you know where you're going once your ship goes under? Which category will your name be in?

_____

_____

_____

_____

_____

Do you feel prepared for eternity?

I encourage you to take your time with these questions. Read Isaiah 55:6-9 and meditate on any additional scriptures the Lord brings to mind.

_____

_____

_____

_____

_____

_____

_____

_____

_____

_____

_____

_____

_____

_____

_____

_____

_____

_____

_____

_____

_____

_____

_____

_____

SEVENTEEN

Access Granted

After worship one Sunday, my pastor made a comment about being permitted to sit at the feet of Jesus. Several hours after that service, I was still pondering this statement. Isn't that interesting ... the thought of being "permitted" to sit at the King's feet? This is the King of the universe we're talking about, and not only do we have permission to sit in His presence, but He calls us *friends*.

How many people would jump at the opportunity to hang out in the White House near the president (even if they aren't a fan of him) or spend the day with a celebrity? Selfie, anyone? How about if they had backstage passes to a special concert or other event, and they got to hobnob with the elite? If not for that special tag around their neck or connection to one of the "important people," they wouldn't be there and yet, because they are, they feel on top of the world!

There's something about having "all access" that we just love, and it's perfectly natural to feel that way. Nonetheless, we put people on pedestals even though they're mere human beings like us.

The only person we should hold in highest regard is the King of the universe, who willingly came down here into *our* mess and always permits us to enter *His* space. Even before His crucifixion and the veil was torn, He was eye-to-eye with us in the flesh … healing us, teaching us, redeeming us, restoring us, loving us, and *washing our feet!*

More importantly, *we* have permission to go before His throne any time, even with our silly human worries and woes, knowing that He's delighted to listen. Nothing we say can make Him love us any less. What a perfect Father He is!

Now here's the really great news: when we accept Jesus as our Savior, and truly live for Him, our backstage passes become eternal—there's no expiration date. We'll have access to new levels of God's glory and timeless treasures to explore all throughout Heaven! Oh, how happy we will be on this never-ending journey spent in the very presence of our Creator. Pastor and author, John Burke, touches on this well in his wonderfully enlightening book, *Imagine Heaven.*

"What glory God will get from basking in his children's discovery of more and more of his wonders. I can imagine searching out the wonders of God's creative beauty for all eternity as an endless act of worship."

Friends, may we never take our grace-based access to the Father lightly.

Read Hebrews 4:16, and journal some of the current issues that have been renting space in your mind. Is it time to bring them before the throne?

_____

_____

_____

_____

Do you ever feel like your access to Jesus is limited? Why or why not? Journal your thoughts.

_____

_____

_____

_____

_____

_____

_____

_____

_____

_____

_____

_____

_____

_____

_____

_____

_____

EIGHTEEN

My Abortion Story and God's Rightful Glory

When it comes to adoption, teen pregnancy, identity issues, and trauma (of several types), I've been there. Some seasons were easier than others, and some left bigger scars. Although each trial provided some incredible gleaning opportunities, sometimes it feels like life has turned into one big, jumbled mess. Yes, it's a mess that has been (and will continue to be) used by God, but the layers of my testimony still often feel overwhelming at times.

However, there's *one* part of my story I didn't think God would *ever* lead me to share publicly. It was the one layer of my soul that I wanted to keep to myself. I've shared it plenty of times in one-on-one (spirit-led) moments, but the overall healing process felt so incredibly sacred, and I wanted to keep it at a more personal level.

Isn't it just like God to always do the opposite of what we

want and sometimes expect? Like inspecting an old attic, He takes a look around at all the pieces of our broken lives and carefully picks up whatever His heart desires. He then lovingly looks us right in the eye—with eyes that pierce straight through our souls—and He calmly asks, *how about we share this with others?*

On the other side of my locked door were the memories of two abortions. I lied to myself for many, many years after making that choice, especially after the second one. Not only did it become a place I wouldn't go, but it became a place that simply didn't *exist*. Facing the truth of that self-inflicted, deeply gut-wrenching pain was way too much to bear, period.

But one day, the Lord impressed on me to take some necessary steps, first by pouring my heart out to Him until it felt empty. I remember it like it was yesterday. As I began talking to Him about my numb suffering, as if He didn't already know, His presence quickly began to fill the space. It felt as if He were physically there with me, embracing me at the top of my basement stairs as I sobbed uncontrollably.

In that moment, I began to receive His unconditional love and completely undeserved grace on a whole new level. I did this heinous thing; I shed innocent blood–the innocent blood of my very own babies ... of *His* babies! Yet, somehow in His unfathomable grace, not only will He still welcome me into Heaven—forgiven—but I get to meet those children there one day! Be still, my shattered heart. I knew He was good, but I wondered, could He really be *this* good?

So quietly, yet so loudly, He spoke to my heart: *Yes, I really am "that" good.* I was totally undone before this Holy, gracious, and compassionate God. All I could do then was cry, and all I can do is cry now. Those waves of grace and mercy that washed over me, left me feeling closer to Him than I ever have. I can't speak for others' situations, of course—but in my case, choosing abortion was purely a matter of selfishness. I knew it. God knew it. Yet, I still wasn't too far from His reach.

Many years later, after that moment on the basement stairs, I found myself pressed for time to find a remote job that was flexible and enabled me to be with my two youngest kids during summer break. While applying to several jobs, each door unapologetically stayed closed.

Suddenly, one door came along and flew so wide open, I thought another day of Pentecost was happening. Just kidding. Still, can you guess what it was? A mostly remote position working for a large pro-life, pro-*woman* nonprofit organization. Part of my job during the (almost) two years I spent there, included speaking at churches and having the opportunity to share my own personal story, which I did. Never in a million years did I think I'd stand on stages one day and openly share how I broke God's heart in this abominable way. At the same time, what an absolute honor it was to testify as living proof of His redeeming love, forgiveness, and mercy.

It felt as if He walked me straight through those doors into that position, and when it was time to leave it, He personally escorted me out. Words can't describe how grateful I am for His perfect sovereignty.

Each day, I stand in awe of Him and His perfect ways. I

stand in awe of the contrast between His holiness and my brokenness. In Romans 7:24-25, Paul says, "What a wretched man I am! Who will rescue me from this body that is subject to death? Thanks be to God, who delivers me through Jesus Christ our Lord!" (NIV). Paul, can you say that again for the people in the back because I am "the people in the back." Even so, my Father holds me *and* my Heavenly babies in the palm of His hand and calls us His own.

What dusty items are hidden away in the attic of your heart? Do you feel God's shining light on those things, calling you to start facing them?

_____

_____

_____

_____

How can you focus on giving Him glory throughout your healing process?

_____

_____

_____

_____

Remember, He is safe, and He is *for* you. Take a deep breath and simply sit at His feet.

The rest will come.

_____

_____

_____

_____

_____

_____

NINETEEN

Dirty VS. Clean

I was about 7 or 8 years old, and our family friend was babysitting me. She was hip, fun, and much older than me, of course. I looked up to her and listening to her talk about boys and life was the ultimate honor in my little eyes. I never once gave a second thought to the fact that she was White.

This particular evening, she called me over to the recliner she was sitting on and asked for my hand. As I gave it to her, she pointed to it with her other hand.

"You see this?" she asked.

"Yes," I said.

"Dirty" was the next word out of her mouth.

She proceeded to point to her own hand and boldly declared it "clean." Then she authoritatively explained by telling me I was "dirty because of the color of my skin, but that she was clean."

My adoptive family was White and had never told me such a thing before—this was new knowledge to me as a kid. I told my mom what my babysitter said to me, and her way of protecting my fragile heart was to brush it off and essentially ignore it. I know my mom meant well. She already had her hands full with all my emotional baggage, not to mention with my wild hair.

More recently, a sweet employee at a retail store asked me a lot of questions about my hair. I answered the questions and was happy to chat. She stopped as I was answering her last question and said, "Oh wait, your hair is real?" I said "yes." She immediately gave me an odd look, looked down at my daughter, and gave her an even nastier look and continued to work. I hoped my daughter didn't notice it, but the second we began walking away, she asked me why she was given such a dirty look. Do you want to know the really sad part? I walked away feeling guilty and sad, like I did something wrong.

While many classify everyone who is partly African American as "Black," our experiences can still differ depending on our shade. Nonetheless, every shade from the lightest to the very darkest is absolutely *beautiful,* and God loves us all the same. It's us humans that are the problem. Just as I have witnessed racism from one side, I've also seen it from the other side. For example, I remember, when my family was on vacation one year, another biracial friend and I decided to go to the movies. As we walked near the theater, a group of other African American girls around our age (12-13), yelled over to us.

"Oh, they think they're cute cause they're light-skinned and got that good hair," they scoffed. They laughed at us. They mocked us. I've always wondered ... Did we do anything to cause that? I was hurt. They didn't even know us!

Another example was when I met a former boyfriend's mom for the first time. She said that she told her son I was too young for him, but "at least I wasn't White." She proudly continued to say that "he could do anything in this world, but he better *never* bring home a White girl."

I know her mindset, upbringing, and culture were completely different from what I had known, but I was floored. After all, I was half White! Those beautiful, caring people who took me in as their own to love and raise me were White! Along those lines, I saw a post recently about a Black woman who joyfully adopted several White children. I couldn't help but wonder, why don't we hear of these situations more often? Why not adopt these innocent White babies and raise them to "not be racist"—for the greater good of society—if so many people personally believe that White people are the problem? Truth be told, we are *all* the problem, and we're doomed outside of Jesus saving us from ourselves. Why shouldn't we cross barriers no matter *what* race a child is? Children are innocent. My mind continued to ponder on the various ways we all could do better, including myself!

Shouldn't we love *all* people as Christians?

In another instance, one of my biological family members (who I had just met at the time) turned to Revelation 1:14, brought it over to me, and said, "just so you always know ...

Jesus was Black! Look, right here, do you see this? Always remember that He was BLACK!"

I remember feeling confused, and not because of the Catholic-style image of Jesus on my parent's bedroom wall, but because I didn't understand why it mattered so much. From the very little I did hear about Jesus up to that point, it sounded to me like He didn't make the impact He made because of the color of His skin. There was so much more to who He was ... *right?*

Yes, racism exists. Yes, we should have healthy and fruitful discussions about it, and yes, we should fight against the injustices (in the right ways). I can't emphasize that enough! My oldest son is Black too, and I can only imagine what other mamas have gone through concerning situations in which race-based police brutality took place. It hurts God's heart so deeply. At the same time, even if my son ever does have a bad experience with a White police officer, he'll still have White grandparents that love him like their own blood, proving that not all White people are "bad." Our jobs, political views, race, etc. don't automatically make us racist any more than our hair colors make us birds. In other words, not *all* White or *all* Black people are racist or anything else for that matter. Generalizing people like this is extremely dangerous, self-destructive, counter productive to society, and just downright unwise. Even more importantly, in this world full of so much noise and deception, we should make sure we are properly educated and cautious about what we believe. The more we research history and God's Word for ourselves, the more we can sharpen one another and make true progress. Going beyond what we are told is absolutely crucial.

Today, I know and declare that I'm a daughter of the King, whose identity is in Him and in Him alone. I live to please the One who created me, not for the approval of others. God is the One—the only One—Who can and does determine that which is "dirty" and "clean." As far as I'm concerned, He has made me new. I forgave that sitter and all others who have hurt or confused me in this area. Sometimes, we're taught certain ways that we don't question until real life smacks us in the face or Christ gets ahold of our hearts.

This is why it's so important to know God on a personal level and live a spirit-led life. Martin Luther King, Jr. was a praying man and was extremely effective in his approach. He also understood that, at the end of the day, the human heart was the issue. It's prideful, and it's deceptive. Even with all the progress King made, we still find ourselves here, long after he's gone. We're so wrapped up in our own issues that many people can hardly sleep at night. We suppress our pain and fears by popping all kinds of pills and spewing hate. The good old days of surviving "hard talks" and coming out stronger and wiser are few and far between.

Make no mistake … These times we're living in are worse than ever and will get worse over time, even if there's small windows of calm in between. Our job, as Christians—as those who have found our identity in Christ—is to act out that identity. Our skin color, heritage, pasts, political views, and everything in between, should *first* fall under that God-given identity. We are sons and daughters of the King before we are Black,White, both or anything else for that matter. Otherwise, we make those things idols (yes, even our race can be made an idol). There's certainly nothing wrong with seeking justice, having passion, and celebrating who God made *you* to be. I teach my kids about their roots (that I know of) and we sometimes watch documentaries and movies in which injustice takes place. We don't only watch ones that pertain to race, but regardless of the context, I usually find myself needing a lot of tissues.

Injustice hurts God, and His tears don't discriminate either. So rather than getting caught up in the giant waves of history and culture, let's unite in our shared humanity and focus on being the hope-filled lighthouses we are called to be.

Have you ever experienced racism first-hand or observed it?

_____

_____

_____

_____

What happened, and how did it make you feel deep down?

_____

_____

_____

_____

Have you ever struggled to accept certain races or other people groups?

_____

_____

_____

Ask God to soften your heart and help you get to the root of this issue.

He'll happily give you His eyes and heart in order to see and love others how He does.

TWENTY

Out Of Order

When I was younger, I used to hate it when my mom made breakfast for dinner. Sure, I ate it, but that was only because I was basically *forced* to eat it (especially if we were out of cereal and no ... cereal isn't for breakfast alone. It's universal, thank you very much). Don't get me wrong, I'm a big fan of this morning meal that causes our senses to jump out of bed before we do, and scream *party time*! Who *can* resist the sight, smell, and sound of sizzling bacon and eggs?

However, the idea of shoving it ahead, well past its famous hours of glory, still feels out of order to me.

There's just something about things being out of order that disturbs the human psyche. I'm reminded of a video my son showed me a few months ago in which a teenage boy was purposely doing things the "wrong way." First, he poured his milk in the bowl *before* his cereal, then he took bites of pizza from the crust end instead of the point. Then, as if it couldn't get any worse, he began biting chunks out of a *whole* KitKat instead of evenly breaking it into bars at the predesignated lines. Are you cringing yet?

Now obviously, *these* things are a matter of environment and culture that began when we were children. After all, if everyone ate pizza from the wrong end, then seeing it done that way wouldn't be so bizarre and make us want to pull our hair out.

Whether right or wrong in our day-to-day habits, we all have a desire for structure and order embedded deep within our souls. Yet so often, we fight it by crying out for disorder, especially in the perilous and delusional culture in which we live. It's like a toddler crying out for something that threatens their wellbeing but are so convinced that it's the end of the world if they don't get their way. Everyone else in the grocery store knows it, too. Outside of what God's Word and Spirit reveals to us, we truly have no clue what's best for us ... just like toddlers don't. History proves this again and again. The hamster wheel may have sped up, but it's still the same old wheel. Oh, how we've forgotten our physical, emotional, and spiritual fragility. It's a dangerous place for mankind to be and a mindset that never ends well.

Disorder literally means confusion, and we all know God is not a God of confusion. Even the Trinity (the Father, Son, and Holy Spirit–three different beings in One) displays a skillful amount of supernatural brilliancy and structure that's gravely under-valued and sometimes deliberately ignored or even denied. Yet, if we truly claim to know God, acknowledging and understanding the basics of the trinity is essential. Creation itself exhibits a great amount of order–if it *weren't* designed with order, we simply wouldn't exist. Our Maker knew exactly what He was doing.

Additionally, we use the saying "out of order" for vending machines, etc. indicating that it's not working properly, right? One or more components are disconnected or broken, rendering it unusable.

Aren't you thankful we serve such a kind and patient God who doesn't leave us when we're feeling out of order? His expectations of us are beyond reasonable, as He covers us in grace and whispers, *you know ... you don't have to shut down. I'm right here.*

The Devil grins as he proudly holds his black sharpie preparing to write an "Out of Order" sign, with plans to smack it on our foreheads. But God has a way of showing up just in time with His tool belt, and He rips the paper up and snaps the sharpie in half. David says in Psalm 8:4, "What is mankind that you are mindful of them, human beings that you care for them?" We're over here making rattling noises and giving out the G4 snack when it's supposed to be J8 ... and yet He still comes and does maintenance on us mere little humans.

I can only imagine what the disciples must have felt when the Son of God washed their crusty, calloused, and dirty feet. My favorite part of this story is the dialogue between Peter and Jesus. As Jesus began to wash Peter's feet, He said, "You do not realize now what I am doing, but later you will understand" (John 13:7). "No," said Peter, "you shall never wash my feet."

Jesus answered, "Unless I wash you, you have no part with me" (John 13:8). "Then, Lord," Simon Peter replied, "Not just my feet but my hands and my head as well!"

Peter enthusiastically welcomed Jesus' maintenance *and* His Heavenly tools–a rag and water. He trusted that His Lord knew the exact order things needed to be done in, even if the very act didn't make sense.

So, no matter how "out of order" life may feel at times, we simply can't go wrong when we trust and prioritize the Creator of order. To make matters even sweeter, one day He will put everything back in His desired and perfect order once and for all!

Do you feel out of order today? Are there any areas of your soul that have a flashing red light indicating something's wrong and requires some holy maintenance?

_____

_____

_____

_____

_____

_____

_____

_____

Heavenly Father,

Oh we love You.

Thank You so much for showing us that every blinking light doesn't mean it's over, and every creaking sound doesn't mean we aren't usable. Your Word is full of underdog stories and true tales of You using the broken in great and mighty ways. Fill my dear sisters (and brothers) reading this with Your everlasting love. Refresh them and help them discover the next level of who and what You call them to be. Help us walk in obedience and humility, always striving to serve others how You did. Keep our souls well-oiled and functioning in a way that pleases You. Reveal to us any areas that need extra maintenance today, and help us to trust Your way of doing things, just like Peter did.

In Jesus' name,

Amen.

TWENTY-ONE

Light in the Darkness: My Prison Ministry Experience

Several years ago, during one of the rare times I watched the news, a man was being put into the back of a police car. The news anchor was dutifully discussing the crime he committed. My eyes filled with tears as I watched footage of him being escorted into that car. It was a completely senseless act of utter evil that left so many hearts broken. And yes, of course this man deserved to pay for his crime … *absolutely*, he did! But to my surprise, I also found myself hurting for him and grieving over his life choices.

I was shocked by the presence of my own tears as they silently rolled down my cheeks. I immediately felt ashamed and wondered what was wrong with me. Who would feel compassion for *this* guy? I realized if I told anyone else this, they would think I was nuts—among other things, I'm sure. After all, society can be merciless toward anyone who breaks the law, especially in the way this man did. People can be just as brutal toward those who advocate for criminals, whether in court or simply in a social media comment as another commenter seeks to understand the unseen layers. Simply put, I felt lonely in my views. However, God didn't judge me, and in that same moment He whispered to my heart, *it's time*.

I knew exactly what He meant. It was time to sign up for prison ministry. It was time to take those feelings of sympathy and put them into action. It was time to acknowledge that God put a growing desire to help them in my heart for a reason.

Soon after facing the facts, I heard a radio ad for Kairos prison ministry. I called that same day and made an appointment to meet with one of the team leaders to go over the necessary information. In a booth at Panera Bread, they unashamedly cried tears of joy as they shared their own personal experiences with those who are incarcerated. I began attending team meetings, which were at a location two hours away. Fortunately, God provided a beautiful, kind woman who lived about 15 minutes from me to be on the same team. She drove me happily to and from each meeting. It was a major blessing because, had she not been there, I can't honestly say I would have committed long-term. The rest of the team was just as amazing as she was. Upon meeting them, I instantly felt a very strong sense of belonging. Prison ministry isn't exactly the most popular type of ministry. So, to fellowship with so many others who shared the same passion, was a blessing and a relief.

After we completed all the team meetings, it was go time. As a team, we would stay together in a local church and then head over to the prison every day for a period of four days. Each day, from early morning to late evening, we would spend time with the all-female inmates or "residents." We shared wisdom with them, laughed with them, cried with them, prayed with them, and even sang with (and to) them.

It was literally one of the best times of my life; truly a "Heaven-meets-earth" moment when you just know you are in the right place at exactly the right time. I learned later that the word *Kairos* means a "propitious moment for a decision or action," which is also interesting. Nonetheless, in those four days, I saw God work in ways I assumed would take years. Not only did He work in the ladies' lives, but He worked in mine as well. I was able to touch a piece of His heart I didn't even know was accessible! The women blessed me immensely, and just like us on the "outside," they all had different life stories filled with various ups and downs. Some were already Christians, eager and ready to learn more as they showed up proudly carrying their Bibles. I saw myself in them, knowing that could have been me if certain life circumstances were different. We all make bad choices as none of us are perfect (read Romans 3:23).

Some of these women's pasts were filled with more pain than others. In fact, one woman's story pierced straight through my heart like a sharp knife through butter. She first arrived at the program reserved and unsure of herself and others. After a day or two of sitting in that atmosphere so heavily saturated in God's love, she courageously walked to the microphone to openly pour out her devastating life story and ask for prayer. Be still my heart. We all showered her with love, including her friends. By the end of the weekend, she laughed and smiled freely, her face glowing. We also sang to them with lyrics along the lines of "you are loved, you are beautiful," and she looked me directly in my eyes as she soaked up every word. My heart ached inside as I wondered if she'd ever been told those things before. It was obvious that the wounded child within her so desperately needed to hear them. I was honored to be one of the people God used in this woman's life, to tell her how He feels about her, despite her past.. It had such an impact on me that I tear up any time I think of her face at that moment. I'll never forget her.

The experience with my fellow team members was just as wonderful. I have never in my life witnessed the body of Christ function so well together. It was a beautiful glimpse of how He calls us all to be, all the time. The bond I shared with each one of them was incredible. As the "inside" team goes into the prison daily, an "outside" team stays behind, praying for us and cooking for us (although we ate in the prison as well). They're also referred to as the prayer and sacrifice team. When we returned to the church each night, they all waited at the door to embrace us. The last night we returned, I was so overwhelmed with joy as I walked through the doorway and saw so many faces I grew to love quickly. I started crying and felt a bit silly about it. The Holy Spirit spoke to my heart, *if you think this is amazing, just imagine Heaven! There will be so many more faces greeting you and celebrating your arrival with an even greater love than this!* Why thank you, Holy Spirit ... that makes me even more emotional.

When my husband picked me back up, I could barely get a word out through all my crying. My heart was arrested by the unfathomable love of God, plain and simple. Thinking of how He allows us these experiences of serving Him, despite our own pasts and current issues, is also incredibly humbling.

I'll forever cherish this experience as well as the merciful and kind Redeemer behind it.

Have you ever had any "Heaven-meets-earth" moments? What's your favorite memory when you recall that experience, and why was it so impactful to you?

_____

_____

_____

_____

_____

What are you passionate about that may feel silly or even scary (at the thought of other people knowing about it)?

_____

_____

_____

_____

Spend some time in prayer, asking the Lord to help you embrace the passions He embedded deep within your soul.

Journal some ways you enjoy being used by Him.

_____

_____

_____

_____

_____

_____

_____

_____

_____

TWENTY-TWO

Hoarders At Heart

Have you ever seen the TV show, *Hoarders?* It documents the difficult challenges real-life hoarders face, as well as the journey they take toward change. Cleaners, organizers, life management specialists, along with friends and family members, work collectively to intervene and help this person. While watching it, I would often think, *Just get everyone out, burn the house to the ground, and start all over.* Forgive me for my extremeness—I'm a clean freak who categorizes and labels the medicine in our bathroom using *clear*, plastic bins. Be that as it may, I still enjoyed witnessing the crazy transformations in these people's homes once all was said and done.

I did eventually stop watching it, however. Seeing those folks suffer as they attempted to justify the act of holding onto each unnecessary item hurt my heart too much. It was truly an agonizing experience for them, and I felt bad. The pure devastation this mental illness causes in their relationships, and lives overall, was also heartbreaking. My soul cringed during every episode.

There are so many issues with hoarding that extend far beyond fire hazards, unpleasant odors, and neighbors' complaints. A hoarder's daily life isn't nearly what it could be due to their attachment to these things that don't even matter. Sure, that certain object had real significance at one point in their lives, but keeping everything causes less and less space for other things and for, well, space. Although they learn how to maneuver between their towers of dusty books and random bicycle wheels every time they walk to the kitchen (if it's even accessible), things don't *have* to be that way.

Learning to adjust to that which is toxic, unwise, and unsafe —rather than getting to the root of it and seeking healing—is one of Satan's greatest tactics. It's a wonderful thing when those who are suffering seek healing and work hard to ensure they don't go back to old habits. This, of course, applies to things seen *and* unseen.

As Christians, many of us also know a thing or two about hoarding (spiritually, that is). How often do we hold onto things or even people when God calls us to let go? Just like the people on the show, we kick, scream, cry, and get angry over it! We desperately grasp for excuses as if our very lives depend on it. Meanwhile, we put our spirits in grave danger when we hoard in our hearts, just like one's home is in danger when they hoard material things. We aren't wired to hold on to unforgiveness, negative memories, past wounds, or ungodly thoughts. Paul, in a letter to the church of Ephesus, says, "Get rid of all bitterness, rage and anger, brawling and slander, along with every form of malice" (v.31). Rather than "get rid of," some versions say, let these things "be removed from you" or "be put away from you." It's clear that there's help readily available, and Paul knew these things were the source of the church's issues. In the following verse, he tells them, "Be kind and compassionate to one another, forgiving each other, just as in Christ God has forgiven you" (Ephesians 4:32). He knew that room for humility and love had to be made before it was too late.

Watching us hold on to so many self-destructive things saddens our Heavenly Father even more than it saddens us when we watch others struggle to let go. He knows life doesn't have to be this way for *us*, and a life full of functionality and freedom awaits us on the other side of our useless piles of junk. In His desire for us to live abundant lives, He wants and deserves to be *our* professional organizer and life specialist who swoops in to "clean house" (pun totally intended). There's no one better for the job! When we allow Him to declutter, we gain more free space in our hearts and in our minds to love, to live, and to worship.

I don't know about you, but I think that sounds like a much more desirable life.

Is there something or someone you're currently struggling to let go of?

_____

_____

_____

_____

Can you remember what was going on in your life when your grip began to tighten on this particular thing or person?

_____

_____

_____

How has your refusal to let go impacted the relationships in your life? How has it impacted your relationship with Jesus?

_____

_____

_____

_____

_____

_____

_____

_____

_____

_____

_____

_____

TWENTY-THREE

"Become Like Little Children..."

I had the honor and privilege of praying over some written prayer requests. These requests were extra special because they were written by young students, including my daughter. Despite its anonymity, I immediately recognized my daughter's card because she faithfully prays for her oldest brother, by name. Her prayers have been so evident in his life as he navigates through the hills and valleys of young adulthood. It's been *incredibly* humbling witnessing God's light break through despite his darkest seasons, to say the least.

Overwhelmed with emotion, I prayed over each card, knowing how precious their faith was in the sight of our Heavenly Father. I'm sure some grieved His heart deeply due to the child's pain and/or fear, and others brought a wide smile to His face as they simply sang praise and thankfulness. Words can't describe the beauty of a prayer request written in child-like handwriting. I've seen, firsthand, how powerful they are, especially when my two youngest children humbly laid their requests before Him on a prayer wall during a difficult season in our lives.

Each request is equally important to God, and I just *know* He holds them tightly next to His heart. After I finished praying over them individually, I prayed that He would guard all their hearts and preserve that childlike faith. The Devil wastes no time coming after our children. The more time he and the world have to indoctrinate and fill them with lies, the easier it can become for them to slip away from the truths they once knew. According to BARNA (a research firm dedicated to providing actionable insights on faith and culture), roughly 70% of high school students who enter college as professing Christians will leave with little to no faith. How heartbreaking this is.

We need to pray harder for our children, and we need to pray God would help restore *our* hearts back to purity. When asked by His disciples "Who then is the greatest in the kingdom of Heaven?" Jesus replied, "Truly I tell you, unless you change and become like little children, you will never enter the kingdom of heaven. Therefore, whoever takes the lowly position of this child is the greatest in the kingdom of heaven. And whoever welcomes one such child in my name welcomes me" Matthew 18:1-5 (NIV).

Being childlike means having no issue walking in faith; being fully and unashamedly dependent on someone else. It means living in constant awe and wonder, and naturally exercising humility and vulnerability. Need I go on? It's no wonder Jesus wants us to become like children!

Oh, and if you're anything like me, you try to do it all. You find yourself carrying a load that's only fit for the cross before you drop it and realize how stupid it was to try that again. Think about it: What does a *child* normally do if they attempt to carry something that's too heavy? What do they do when they simply don't *want* to carry something–whether heavy or not? They ask, "Can *you* carry this?" Without a second thought, they pass the burden right off as they run, jump, or skip away in complete freedom, ready for the next adventure as if the burden never existed at all.

My prayer for you and I today is that we become more like children.

-May we consistently walk in the purest of faith and remember our constant need for the Father.

-May we always live in awe and wonder, soaking up each moment in life for all it's worth.

-May we seek to live humbly and vulnerably as we quickly pass our burdens off to our Daddy so we can run freely.

Which one of the childlike ways listed above do you feel you struggle with the most? Set aside some quiet time to pray and focus on those characteristics with the leading of the Holy Spirit.

_____

_____

Make plans to do something fun within the next four weeks. You can go alone, or with friends or family, but make sure it's something that makes you feel young again. Whatever it is, don't hesitate to act silly, have fun, and laugh while you're at it. If you're a parent or grandparent, I'm sure your kids/grandkids will be blessed by this, too. Just because our bodies become stiff over time, doesn't mean our personalities have to.

TWENTY-FOUR

You're God's Favorite

My two youngest kids and I love to goof around. Phrases like, "Whoever goes upstairs and gets my charger is my favorite kid" and "Whoever goes and turns the bathroom light off is my favorite kid" are totally normal in this house. They love to laugh and shove each other as they race on this mission of achieving the golden, nonexistent, *favorite child* trophy. After one of their 'commissions,' my then 9-year-old son teased, "you can only have *one* favorite, Mom!" Even though we were still in silly mode, I told him I equally admire everything about him and his siblings as wonderfully unique individuals. I explained that no matter what any of them do in life ... the good, the amazing, the bad, and the ugly–they will *all* always be my favorite.

Having that conversation with him resurrected memories of another discussion I had with a relative several years ago. One day, she said that she didn't feel special enough to God because there was a sea of others Jesus died for too, not just her. She wanted His love to be radically specific to her; She wanted to feel like *she* was His "favorite." We all tend to humanize Him like this, at times.

Thankfully though, God isn't like one of those dads on reality shows with three times more kids than the minivan can fit, and He surely isn't limited on the amount of time and attention He can give to each child. He leans into the sounds of our voices, catches our tears in a bottle, and knows the exact number of hairs on our heads. He never misses a game, birthday, or important performance. While pondering the pure majesty of our God, David writes in Psalm 8:4, "What is mankind that you are mindful of them, human beings that you care for them?" We are the apple of our very Creator's eye (which David also shares further along, in Psalm 17:8). Isn't that something?

The only favoritism God ever shows is in unison with His beloved creation. At the same time, His relentless love, forgiveness, grace, and compassion is distinctively specific to every single one of us. Let that soak in. Some of us have been adopted into His Heavenly family by choosing to receive and embrace His sacrifice, but His Word says He desires that *none* should perish. All He has to offer is open to anyone who will take it. No one must stand outside, looking in through the window and feeling left out. This is what makes God the perfect Daddy: His ability to be omniscient and omnipresent. Knowing us at the very core of our innermost being, He has and *is* everything we need. He always has our best interest at heart too, even when we don't know what's best for ourselves.

Do you ever have a hard time believing you're the apple of God's eye? No, seriously ... like *really* believing it in the depths of your soul? Journal your thoughts.

_____

_____

_____

_____

What is/was your relationship like with your earthly father? In what ways does that closeness, brokenness, or absence directly affect the way you see your Heavenly Dad?

_____

_____

_____

_____

Research verses pertaining to how God "delights in us." Study the context as well then jot down your favorite one.

_____

_____

_____

_____

_____

_____

_____

_____

_____

TWENTY-FIVE

Insta-sham

Most mornings, when it's not chaotic, the kids and I read this awesome devotional by Max Lucado called *How Great is our God*. It's full of fun and interesting facts—some of which I never knew (okay, *all* of which I never knew). The facts are followed by a sweet little life lesson and a simple prayer. After we complete our reading, we move on to our *Merriam-Webster's Word of the Day* book. Both readings usually lead us down virtual rabbit trails as we seek to learn more about our current topic.

Our most recent rabbit trail began when we learned the word *pareidolia,* "the tendency to see a specific or meaningful image in a random visual pattern." The definition included a neat example: the Pedra da Gávea, a 2,700-foot-high mountain in Brazil's Tijuca Forest that some say has the appearance of a human face in it. Naturally, we Googled the mountain to see this supposed formation for ourselves. Instead, we were met with various images of individuals who were happily (but very dangerously), hanging off the edge of the same small, pointy cliff, the vastness of the blue ocean filling up the background. Upon looking at the first image, anxiety set in as if the photos were going to come to life, and I was about to witness them fall to their deaths. *Goodness gracious, these people are absolutely nuts,* I thought. *Don't they know God gave us life as a gift?*

Upon scrolling through more photos and reading additional information, I found that it's all an illusion. While there *are* real people out there who love living on the edge (no pun intended) for the sake of posting anxiety-producing Instagram photos (and giving us folks on the other side of the screen heart attacks), that wasn't the situation here. It's a sham … a sham that is based simply on angles. Some people wait for up to six hours in line for their turn to hang from the "risky" cliff, wearing their biggest smiles. The pictures really are neat. I may even do it myself if I ever have the privilege of visiting Rio. Nonetheless, these seemingly horrifying photos are based entirely on *deception.* Much like the false images from the Deceiver himself.

Do you ever fall for the false images Satan presents to you? We all do at times, but *which* lies of his do you believe the most? You're not smart enough? Not beautiful enough or not skinny enough? Not a good enough mom? Perhaps you believe God could never forgive you for your sins?

They say a picture is worth a thousand words. Well, Satan would love nothing more than for us to believe all the antibiblical words that his distorted pictures speak. He wants us to completely absorb them as concrete truth and unchangeable reality.

I can't tell you how many times I've believed something to be true, that wasn't. I'd gullibly listen to the lies Satan planted in my mind because, after all, the "facts" were right there. I could practically see it for myself! Just like those cliff photos, he was presenting a false truth. It was a counterfeit replica based on pure trickery. Out of God's unfailing love, the Holy Spirit would whisper to my heart, *look a little closer, there's more than meets the eye. Not everything is as it seems.*

Then after I climbed down from my throne of stubbornness, the layers of fog would lift. The truth peeked its head out, and I was left feeling like an idiot. Honestly, I've been very humbled by those eye-opening moments. I'm still learning to slow down before jumping the gun.

Friend, it's time we start investigating these images and stop believing any old thing that comes into our minds. Our culture is filled with poisonous lies lurking around every corner, seeking to destroy our souls. The enemy sure knows how to make them look good too! He's the master of illusion, and it all began with tweaking the image of truth in the Garden of Eden.

Remember, God is not just God over reality and truth, He *is* truth! Let's hold on to that fact like our lives depend on it ... because they do.

. . .

Journal some thoughts about why you think the truth in and of
itself is so powerful.

_____

_____

_____

_____

Why is it dangerous to believe we each can create and follow our own absolute truth?

_____

_____

_____

_____

_____

Here are three verses to consider, but I encourage you to look up additional ones and include them in your journaling:

"But when he, the Spirit of truth, comes, he will guide you into all the truth. He will not speak on his own; he will speak only what he hears, and he will tell you what is yet to come." (John 16:13)

"God is spirit, and his worshipers must worship in Spirit and in truth." (John 4:24)

"Jesus answered, 'I am the way and the truth and the life. No one comes to the Father except through me.'" (John 14:6)

_____

_____

_____

_____

_____

_____

_____

TWENTY-SIX

The Real GOAT

When it comes to what's currently "in," I'm a little behind (okay, *really* behind). My soul can't help but crave the movies, music, and TV shows from decades before my time. Despite the issues within those times, there's something about those previous eras that made simplicity shine in a way that seems lost today. I feel like life is rushing by in one swift motion, full of colorful blurs. It seems there's a new style, a new iPhone, and new slang words every few seconds. (Wait, is slang even a word anymore?) Words that once meant one simple thing, are now being given completely new and different definitions. Who can keep up?

After hearing one certain slang word several times, but never quite caring enough to figure it out, someone told me what the word "GOAT" means. If you're anything like me, I should tell you I am not referring to Old MacDonald's goats. In fact, this rather cool acronym means "Greatest Of All Time."

For instance, Simone Biles is considered the "GOAT" of gymnastics and now even sports a diamond-encrusted pendant shaped like a goat. Learning this term of endearment immediately made me think of Jesus. Okay, maybe you're rolling your eyes and thinking it's cliché, but how could I *not* be reminded of Him? We seem to forget that even celebrities are made of "dust" just like we are, and all the outstanding things they do only exist because the greater GOAT exists—the GOAT Who *created* GOATS. Please be careful not to trip over that mic I just dropped.

Think about these things:

- Jesus existed even before the beginning of time.
- He came to Earth, born to a virgin, and gave hope to the hopeless.
- He performed miracle after miracle and exemplified a type of love that was totally foreign to the world.
- He lived sinlessly.
- He fulfilled incredible prophecies in great detail.
- He boldly challenged religious leaders and their wide-spread traditions.
- He died (as He said He would) and came back to life (exactly *when* He said He would).

Not to mention, there were numerous witnesses of His life,

death, and resurrection, plus all it entailed. Many of these witnesses died, or were willing to die, for their faith in Him. That's how convinced they were after encountering Him in one way or another. To top it off, there were no viral videos reaching mass audiences and no quick transportation to travel. Yet, His ministry lasted for only three short years. He was crucified around 2,000 years ago, and we are *still* talking about Him. That speaks *volumes!* Need I go on?

Maybe we can even take that acronym a step further and call Him "God Over All Things." Still the GOAT, still the King of kings.

Our human hearts want so desperately to hold someone up— to personally identify with that sports team or musician. It enables our inner underdog to gain a tidbit of temporary satisfaction. It's normal! There's also nothing wrong with these cultural terms that give honor where honor is due.

Nonetheless, there is only *One* Who deserves all the honor and glory simply because, and He happens to be the same One who loves and validates the underdog in a way nothing and no one else ever could. Our Savior is truly the greatest *everything* of all time and I'll forever, unashamedly scream that from the rooftops.

Did you ever stop and think about what a big deal Jesus really is? Again, there's nothing wrong with us admiring others at times, but we must keep the proper perspective of our Savior. As I share this, I'm reminded of Colossians 1:16 … "For in him all things were created: things in heaven and on earth, visible and invisible, whether thrones or powers or rulers or authorities; all things have been created through him and for him." Isn't this such a beautiful verse?

Spend some time researching Jesus from a historical standpoint. It doesn't have to be extensive research, of course, but explore prayerfully and see what you find.

Journal your findings and ask the Holy Spirit to help you grow
in reverence for our Savior.

_____

_____

_____

_____

_____

_____

_____

_____

_____

_____

_____

_____

_____

_____

_____

_____

_____

_____

_____

_____

_____

_____

TWENTY-SEVEN

VeggieTales All Day, Baby

"Isn't that somewhat babyish for a kid his age? Do you have anything that's a little more mature for him?"

An employee at the Christian bookstore had suggested the VeggieTales series for my then seven-year-old son (who's now approaching 21). Talking vegetables and silly songs? My son was way too old for that…

Oh, if only I could go back in time. I would have purchased every VeggieTales DVD they had for him. You see, this employee knew something I didn't know as a young believer: the importance of preserving your child's spiritual and emotional innocence in a world full of visual garbage. At the time, I didn't have anyone guiding me as a Christian parent.

I've since learned that what may look "babyish" in the eyes of the world, is often what's best for the child in a culture where even *food* commercials are sexualized. The Devil is real, and he wants our children ... badly. Schools, the entertainment industry, libraries, and more have all become perniciously infiltrated with anti-God concepts as the norm. Just look around. Even many TV shows targeted toward *toddlers* have horribly inappropriate messages that seek to brainwash these children toward certain lifestyles (that they might not choose otherwise if it weren't for it constantly being shoved down their throats).

I used to classify believers with this perspective as "weirdo Christians who over-spiritualize everything", but now I understand. While God has—and will always have—the victory, Satan is still the "prince of the air." Therefore, evil *is* truly all around us, even in that which presents itself as innocent and harmless. 1 Peter 5:8 tells us to "Be alert and of sober mind. Your enemy the devil prowls around like a roaring lion looking for someone to devour." (NIV)

Thankfully, we serve a God who is greater than any evil that may abound, meaning we don't have to walk in fear. At the same time, it's crucial we don't water down the importance of walking in wisdom and awareness. Everything our Heavenly Dad tells us in His word is for a reason, and it's not only for our own good and protection, but for the good and protection of others as well. Again, just take a look around ... it's become clearer than ever that we need to cling to Him and discard anything that attempts to exalt itself against Him.

After all, our culture's agenda isn't just about prematurely exposing our children to adult ideologies, or simply helping them "embrace themselves and others." It's about corrupting, changing, and perverting their precious little minds with lies and confusion about God, His creation, and their very own identities. God's truth initially comes naturally to a child until we rip it away from them, not even realizing the true depths and eternal consequences of what we're really doing. In fact, our world has grown so dark that when you *do* encounter a child who has age-appropriate understanding, or a parent who understands the value and importance of guarding their child (in healthy ways), they're viewed as the oddball. In other words, instilling Godly principles and basic morality in our children, which is honorable, has become a strange thing in many people's eyes.

By no means am I saying we should put our kids in a bubble or stifle their emotional growth. Just recently, after hearing about another school shooting, I talked with my two youngest children again concerning what to do in the event of an emergency. Sure, this shouldn't even *have* to be a conversation and yet, it does. It's the sad reality of the fallen world in which we live. We couldn't hide it from them even if we tried, but we can seek to have balance and wisdom as we navigate.

Now, of course I'm no expert. Other than "Mom," I don't have any fancy titles associated with my name concerning children unless "former nanny" or "youth leader" counts too. Nevertheless, I'm sharing all of this from plenty of experience, what's been revealed to my heart, many parenting books, and other research I've done over the years, dating back to high school. I've learned a lot about what *not* to do as well. I have to ask the Lord for help with parenting on a regular basis, but simply put, I'm passionate about this because I love kids!

Let's allow them to blow bubbles and enjoy entertainment that's created for *children* with wholesome messages that don't weave in political digs or the occult. Even if they're older than the average audience the show was produced for, so what! When I was about eight or nine years old, one of my friend's parents took us to visit another family. All of us kids were in the basement watching TV. When I asked if we could watch something other than *Winnie the Pooh*, I'll never forget those kids refusing to change the channel and saying it's all they were allowed to watch. My little unfiltered self probably wanted to watch *Child's Play* or something. God bless those parents and their children for unapologetically guarding their home in a way that worked best for their family—even if those decisions didn't make sense to others. I don't believe those kids *literally* only watched *Winnie the Pooh*, but even as a child, I understood that their parents were involved and filtered what was and wasn't allowed in their home.

If *you* weren't defended or protected as a child, whether in physical ways, spiritual/emotional ways or both—take it to your Heavenly Daddy. Allow Him to be the adult you needed in those moments to guard your spirit and help you process those tough and confusing emotions.

Lastly, if you feel *you've* failed to protect your own child(ren) in ways you believe you should have, and you're living in shame, stop it! There is no perfect parent but God alone, and all that matters is that we make necessary changes, when and where we can, moving forward. During a recent double date, while chatting about marriage and life, one of our dear friends said, "My goal is to only make new mistakes." What a great word; simple and yet so very profound. As imperfect humans in a very fallen world, we'll always make mistakes … it's inevitable. Being intentional and diligent in trying not to repeat the same ones is wise.

Our children, teens, and young adults can easily sense whether a parent's, guardian's, teacher's, or other leader's love is genuine, and when they're trying to do and be better for the child's sake. Trust, respect, and credibility are established.

If your children are older and you feel you "damaged" them, or there's no hope for healing in the relationship, ask God for help. Sure, the answers don't always come in the way we'd like them to, but He can certainly lead us in the right directions at the right times.

So, let's protect our babes fiercely, while also giving ourselves grace for the many, *many* times we'll mess up along the way.

What were you exposed to at a young age that deeply affected you? How do you think this made God feel? Are you ready to begin praying for healing? Why or why not?

_____

_____

_____

_____

_____

Was there ever a time (or lots of times) in which you felt forced into adulthood prematurely and didn't have the freedom to feel and behave as the child you were? Whatever it is, be completely honest with yourself and with God. Again, He's the only perfect parent that ever existed, and He's eager to wrap His loving arms around *you*!

_____

_____

_____

_____

Is there any aspect of your parenting in which you feel you could use some help? There's no shame in seeking mentorship, counseling, and/or advice from others. Consider laying it before God and seeing which direction He leads you in.

_____

_____

_____

_____

_____

_____

_____

_____

_____

_____

TWENTY-EIGHT

Seek and You Shall Find

My first car was a 1995-ish red Mercury Sable, and that bad boy was my heart. The first thing I did when I got it, was head straight to the Christian bookstore to buy some cheesy accessories for it. I settled on a colorful air freshener to hang from my mirror that had 1 Corinthians 2:9 on it and a blue Jesus bumper sticker. I was proud and unashamed. My bumper sticker, in my opinion, unapologetically showed others my love for the One who rescued my soul. Representing Him was the very least I could do. I believed (and still believe) that God can and *does* use little things to get our attention, and these simple declarations were important to me. Who knows ... perhaps when I'm in Heaven, I'll get to meet someone who benefited from seeing that sweet name on my old clunker at just the right moment.

I wonder what would be displayed on Jesus' car if He lived

in our times. Maybe it would be a *"Follow Me"* decal or a *"Don't drink and drive ... if you were at the wedding in Cana"* bumper sticker (I'm kidding). Either way, no matter how well designed, creative, or clever, all of our proudly plastered declarations are, none could ever hold a match to Jesus and His immutable truth. I'm not saying decals, stickers, and signs are *bad*—I'm a Jesus bumper sticker girl myself, remember? All I'm saying is that usually those of us who are the "loudest" seem to be searching and hungry for something deeper without always realizing it. We feel the need to let complete strangers know where we stand on every matter, sometimes all at once. It's no longer just a political or spiritual statement here or there, it's *everything* in between and then some. Our stickers and decals loudly scream, *this is who I am, this is what I support, this is who or what I love, and this is who or what I hate.* It feels like our excessive need to tout our personal views is another symptom of an inner desire to be known. This confusion can be observed on social media as well. It's not uncommon to see a post written about someone's late loved one being in a better place, only to say in their next post that they're still an Atheist. Yet, according to Atheists, there is no better place. Clearly, so many people aren't sure *what* they believe. Something sounds good, seems to make sense, and others confirm, so we jump on the bandwagon and let the rest of the world know. Even us Christians lose our way at times too. Satan is the master of blurring lines.

With so many lies thrown at us from the media and entertainment industry, society fails to stop and think for itself anymore. It's like being force fed so quickly that we can't even taste what we're chewing—yet we allow it. Pride grows so big that there's often no room left for the genuine humility it takes to do personal soul searching.

This is so unfortunate because a seeking heart is a major threat to the kingdom of Hell. Former new ager and host of *Heaven and Healing* podcast, Angela Ucci said in an interview, "if you're searching hard enough for the truth, you'll eventually run into Jesus." Essentially, former new agers, just like Angela, were already seeking the way, the truth, and the life … and so they found Him. In John 14:6, Jesus says, "I am the way and the truth and the life. No one comes to the Father except through me." In the end, the power wasn't in their crystals or incense, it came through their seeking.

There's a smorgasbord of viewpoints and belief systems claiming to be the truth and ultimate path to peace, but Jesus and everything He stands for is the only solid solution to every issue. Despite how some may feel about the word "only," He really is the *only* way to God and the *only* One that can satisfy our wicked and weary human hearts. "Only" never sounded so good—there's life-changing freedom in our searching when it's linked to the name of Jesus! One day, every knee will bow and every tongue confess that Jesus Christ is Lord, according to Philippians 2:10-11. The Bible's trustworthy pages are filled with words more powerful and more profound than any words we could ever see on political signs, bumper stickers, water bottles, or anywhere else! Sure, those material things can still plant seeds and even open doors for conversation with strangers,

but the living Word of God being written on our hearts is what
matters the most. (Read 2 Corinthians 3:3 and 2 Corinthians
5:20.)

May we continue to seek, find, and represent Jesus no matter
the cost.

Reflect back on when you first came to know Jesus on a
personal level. Did you have a history of dabbling in anything
that sounded good? Who or what helped you drown out all the
worldly noise before you realized the truth? How does looking
back on that time in your life (knowing God saw your heart and
rescued you from the lies) make you feel? Journal your
thoughts.

What messages do you want others to see and read when they
look at you and your life? It may sound like a cliché or surface-
level question, but I want you to really think about it. Are there
specific attributes of God that you're passionate about
highlighting? Do you simply want people to take note of His
power through how radically He turned your life around?

_____

_____

_____

_____

Pray, then assemble a list of all the messages you want your
story to speak.

_____

_____

_____

_____

_____

_____

As long as your heart and walk is in obedience to His will, He'll take care of all the "hows."

TWENTY-NINE

Dirty Dogs Without Christ

Getting our black and white pup was such a blessing, even though I usually prefer cats if I really had to choose (though, I love *all* animals). We had wanted a puppy for quite some time, especially after we had just gone through a hard season in our lives. So, as you can imagine, the kids were ecstatic when someone told us about nearby puppies that were up for adoption.

When the kids and I first met up with his previous owner to meet him, my son noticed a car parked near ours that was covered inside and out with Snoopy memorabilia. The puppy's name was fitting to his coloring: "Snoopy." So, we happily kept that name once he was officially ours. In fact, we didn't just *keep* the name, we ran with it. He has a stuffed Charlie Brown that we found at a local Goodwill, and more recently, a stuffed Snoopy that we *also* found at Goodwill (might I add, that one was brand spankin' new)! I also made him a little red Snoopy house that he would go into when we'd tell him to "go home." Clearly, our fur babe is a spoiled little stinker.

Last winter, after giving him a bath and drying him back into a ball of fluff, I took him outside. To my surprise, up against the sparkling white snow, he suddenly wasn't so perfectly white anymore. In fact, he looked *dirty!*

Beyond the disappointment my disturbed inner clean freak was feeling, I couldn't help but think about how dirty we are in comparison to such a holy and pure God.

It's easy to wash ourselves with the lies that we're so squeaky clean, especially compared to the Karen we just witnessed yelling in the grocery store parking lot. The reality is, we can also be some dirty dogs! We could never come close to the purity of our Heavenly Father unless we're washed by *His* very own hands and with *His* very own son's blood. He never misses a spot. We are only made righteous through Him and Him alone.

That precious, sanctifying blood makes us acceptable in His sight, and we don't ever have to worry about Him cringing over how dirty we look. Talk about good news!

Read Isaiah 64:6 and Isaiah 1:18. How do these truths make you feel?

_____

_____

Do you ever feel that your sins aren't as bad as others'? Read
Luke 18:10-14 and journal your thoughts.

_____

_____

_____

_____

_____

_____

_____

_____

_____

_____

_____

_____

_____

_____

_____

_____

_____

_____

_____

_____

_____

_____

THIRTY

Pilgrim's Progress

If you're not familiar with the captivating allegory *The Pilgrim's Progress*, I strongly recommend looking it up. It tells the story of a character named Christian who goes on a laborious journey to the Celestial City with the hopes of getting the metaphorical (but very literal) burden off his back. I won't give too much away in case you haven't seen it and would like to read or watch it. I will, however, share that this increasingly difficult expedition is filled with numerous ups and downs. Each obstacle represents some of the different tactics, snares, and distractions Satan uses to get us off the path that leads to God … the only path that leads to true freedom. While the allegory itself plays out in a way some may consider a little elementary, the principles and truths represented within it are biblical and *incredibly* profound. It's truly a beautiful and brilliant work of art.

As I recall the various elements Christian faced throughout his journey, I think of my own voyage through life. It feels as if I've spent an immeasurable amount of time trekking through treacherous terrain and sinking in quicksand. There were times when I was crawling (rather than walking), and there were times when I simply wasn't on the path at all. So often, I was tempted to believe the lie that I couldn't do it anymore. I wanted to curl up in a ball on the side of the trail like a little child; refusing to take another step. Yet, the Lord always showed up again and again to remind me He's still in control, and He allows pain for His glory and for my good. He was with me every step of the way, even during the moments when I've felt completely abandoned.

I'm also reminded of Joseph's journey... my favorite story in the Old Testament. If you see my Bible, it would be easy to tell as these pages in Genesis are filled with triple the hearts, highlights and notes. It looks like a teenager's diary in the 80s. Despite the unfair difficulties Joseph faced throughout his life, it was continuously evident that God never left his side. Scripture even says several times that "the Lord was with him." Joseph faithfully stayed the course, and that enabled God to continue covering him with favor. In the end, all the pieces of his life came together as one beautiful tapestry—even more colorful than the elaborate coat his father gave him. This beauty testified to God's sovereignty and the fact that He can overcome (and use) that which is evil, for the sake of fulfilling His purposes in our lives. In fact, while chatting with his fearful and remorseful brothers, Joseph said, "Am I in the place of God? You intended to harm me, but God intended it for good to accomplish what is now being done, the saving of many lives. So then, don't be afraid" (Genesis 50:20 NIV).

Cearly, it doesn't matter if evil things were unjustly imposed on us like in Joseph's case, or if it was caused by our very own decisions and actions; God can use it all!

Maybe you're walking slowly down your path, flinching at every noise you hear in the nearby trees. Maybe you're proudly wearing your freshly polished armor of God as you skip down your path, praising the Lord and double-dog daring the Devil to try you. Perhaps you've fallen off a cliff and are currently underwater, replaying your whole life through your mind as your lungs begin to burn. That's when Satan convinces you this is the end. If that's you, please believe me when I say, I can wholeheartedly relate.

No matter where we are on our individual paths to the "Celestial City," one thing is for sure: We need to help each other along the way. We all (and I do mean *all*) need Jesus during every moment of this up-and-down adventure called life. My friend, those noises within the trees... aren't just the wind blowing. There's real danger out there, which could become eternal and irreversible should you leave the path for good. Those detours that promise alternative relief for our souls outside of Christ? They aren't the least bit trustworthy. We must stay on the path, eyes upward at all costs.

What burdens are on your back today?

What obstacle along your journey feels impossible to overcome? Perhaps you're just tired from all the traveling and believe you don't have it in you to continue. You're right—you don't, but we know Someone Who does, and that *Someone* sure loves it when we surrender ourselves. That's when He really starts rolling up His sleeves.

_____
_____
_____
_____
_____
_____
_____
_____
_____
_____
_____
_____
_____
_____
_____
_____
_____
_____

When you have some down time, consider watching and/or reading *The Pilgrim's Progress,* then spend some time with the Lord in prayer.

Evaluate your own journey thus far.

Ask Him for continued guidance, and most importantly, give Him thanks for bringing you as far as He has already. He's not finished with you yet!

THIRTY-ONE

Beyond The Surface

When our daughter was five years old, she started having nightmares. These episodes lasted for two years straight. Every night, around 3 AM—like clockwork—she would drowsily wander into our room to let us know she had another nightmare. In fact, some of them were so intense they would affect her during her waking hours if something reminded her of them.

This was during a time when God started opening my eyes to the supernatural and deliverance. A woman I knew told me my daughter had a spirit of fear living inside of her. Through a series of conversations, I realized the nightmares started after my husband and I watched the movie *JAWS* while my daughter was in the room. While it's certainly nothing like the unbelievably graphic movies of today, my daughter was still way too young at that time to see it (she was also very sensitive, which made the situation much worse). I know this all might sound crazy, believe me! But this was our experience.

I walked my daughter through a simple deliverance prayer, and from that day forward, she's been nightmare free for four years and counting! The proof was in the pudding. God bless that woman for lovingly explaining how to grab the bull by the horns and help my daughter get free from that ongoing issue once and for all.

Evil spirits love nothing more than an "unattended child" or a child who is not being covered in prayer or protected. We personally prayed for our kids etc. but still clearly had some blind spots. Kids are helpless and vulnerable, so it's easy for unclean spirits to manipulate and deceive them. These spirits jump at any open door, even if the child didn't necessarily do anything wrong. I'm reminded of when I was in 2nd or 3rd grade. Any time a particular friend and I were alone, I would twist her arms until she cried … then I'd beg her not to tell. There was no reason for it, but I had this unexplainable inner desire to hurt her. Looking back to that time, I now see I was absolutely filled with rage, among other spirits. Sadly, this is so much more common than people realize, but we quickly water the behavior down and attempt to explain it away.

Have you ever met a child who was as sweet as pie, and you just *knew* they had a special anointing on them? And yet, you've also noticed that this same child can be filled with an insurmountable amount of rage and anger at the drop of a hat … as if "something else" took over? Before I continue, let me pause here and stress that it's not *always* due to spirits.

Sometimes the child may have other issues going on, or may even be going through a tough time emotionally, resulting in them acting out. They need love, adequate attention, security, understanding, and age-appropriate communication to help them through those difficult times. Other times, it might simply be a matter of needing specialized help from someone who's properly trained to deal with their particular problems. But as for the cases that *are* spiritual at the root, it's devastatingly heartbreaking how so many adults, and sometimes other children, judge and shun these kiddos for their questionable behaviors. No child in and of themselves, wants to be a terror; it's not their fault (and unclean spirits love nothing more than keeping their influence hidden). With that said, rather than gossiping about them or writing them off as the "bad kid," we should be praying for them and showing them the Christ-like love they so desperately need! This is especially true for those who are in positions of authority over children.

I'm reminded of a TV series I watched several years ago that centered around inmates and their childhoods. One man shared that when he was only six years old, he was locked in the trunk of a car and starved. Prior to this (and even in the years following this incident), he landed in the hands of many different abusers—over and over again. He shared how excited he was to eventually be adopted by this one particular man because he was a well-known pillar in the community. He figured that he'd finally be safe and loved; his little heart so desperately wanted an adult in his life that he could trust. Well, that "upstanding guy" ended up abusing him too, depleting what little hope he had left. Many years and several crimes later, he's now spending his life in a prison.

Demons flock to these and other psychological fractures because they know that if there's enough trauma, they can more easily influence the child throughout their entire lives. Obviously, the example above is an extreme case, but abuse is all around us, and these things go so much deeper than meets the eye.

I believe when God sends hurting kids (young or old) into a Christian's path, it's because He knows they need our love and prayers. After all, Jesus loved children! This merciless world is so eager to chew our children up and spit them out. The harshness of reality always happens naturally, without fail. It certainly doesn't need our help.

Our job is to *combat* the darkness, and we can only do that by being a light in their lives in whatever way(s) God calls us.

Even saying the simplest kind words goes such a long way. I sure remember what it was like when an adult was kind toward me as a child (and even more so when one was rude). You don't forget those things! It's so important to bend down eye-to-eye and make these kids feel safe, seen, and heard—*no matter* their story.

Let's pray fervently for Heavenly insight. Discerning what's beyond the surface will help us love them better, pray for them more specifically, and guard them wisely (when it's our job to). They deserve to enjoy the childhood and adolescence God so sweetly gifted to them.

Have you ever seen a story on TV or even witnessed a situation that concerned cruel and sinister behavior in a child? Did you feel like there was more to it than met the eye?

_____

_____

_____

_____

_____

Dedicate a day or two to praying for local schools, daycares etc. and don't forget to pray for parents too. Also, consider creating a prayer list just for the children in your life.

_____

_____

_____

_____

_____

_____

_____

_____

_____

_____

_____

_____

Book recommendation for helping children understand deliverance:

The Little Skunk, by Sue Banks

THIRTY-TWO

Real or Counterfeit?

My youngest son and I recently watched a neat YouTube video in which an American man was visiting an African village, bringing various types of candy. It was the first time these villagers tried anything so sweet. Upon realizing a wrapper stood in the way of him and the mysterious treat, one man unashamedly pulled out his large knife and cut through it like a champ. If I could have jumped through the TV and given him a fist pump, I would have.

As these folks curiously tried each foreign and brightly colored piece of candy, their reactions were priceless. Some loved them, and others didn't like them at all. In fact, one woman said Twizzlers taste like plastic. She didn't seem to understand what all the hype was about.

In their defense, these people are professional hunters; they eat directly from the earth on a daily basis. There are no factories adding chemicals and other preservatives to their plates. In other words, their palates went from tasting nature in its purest forms to tasting strange textures and sour flavors. When you're so used to the real thing, everything else becomes ... well, junk. So much of our processed foods cause obesity, chronic diseases, and a plethora of other health issues. I know all too well the damage overly processed foods cause our bodies, *believe me!* Getting my own health in order has been quite a struggle. Fortunately, food that *God* made (whole foods) often works as medicine as it heals, restores, and energizes. It's authentic, "real" food.

Speaking of authenticity, I once heard that many bank tellers are easily able to spot fake money, not just because of the little clues, but because they handle *real* money on a regular basis. Therefore, when something fake comes through their fingers, they're more inclined to recognize it as a counterfeit.

This makes me wonder ... How many "fake things" does Satan try to bring across *our* hands, eyes, or ears? He takes everything God made and seeks to pervert it by making his own counterfeit version. Personally speaking, I fell for his versions more often than I care to admit. Nevertheless, He simply can't destroy God or the authenticity and power of His truth (the only absolute truth). All he can do is attempt to replicate it, mock it, and ultimately mislead and deceive people.

There is no value in a fake. Imagine going to a pawn shop to sell a ring you were cunningly told was worth a million dollars. Can you picture yourself making life decisions based on the value you believe is within your possession, only to find out it was all based on a lie? Falling for that lie would lead to disappointment, embarrassment, and empty pockets. When we fall for Satan's lies and counterfeits, we're left with dire consequences …. consequences that lead to Hell in the end if we live unrepentant lives. There is no walking out of Hell's doors like you would a pawn shop. Once the door is closed behind you, that's *it*. Our Heavenly Father wants us to be so close to Him, we only crave what's good, real, and edifying to our spirits. That way, when counterfeit things do come along, we immediately recognize their damaging repercussions and refuse to ingest it.

Settling for nothing less than God's version will always, without fail, make a positive impact on our friends, families, and communities. Of course, we won't get it right every time because we are human, but we can certainly live our lives trying and getting better each day! It's time we spit the plastic out and "Taste and see that the Lord is good" (Psalm 34:8).

How is your spiritual palate? Is it trained to immediately recognize what's real vs. fake?

_____

_____

_____

_____

_____

_____

THIRTY-THREE

When God Winks

Well, I finally did it … I went somewhere I've been wanting to go for several years (no, like *really* wanted to go). Do you know where? Lean in close … a little closer … okay, that's good. I went to a museum! Yes, you read that right, but I'm not talking about just *any* old museum, I'm talking about the Creation Museum and the Ark Encounter. This wonderful adventure to Kentucky may seem simple or even silly, but it's been a dream of mine. The Lord knew just the perfect time to allow me to experience it too.

Both the Ark Encounter and Creation Museum, which are located about 45 minutes away from one another, are incredible. So, as someone who thinks the *world* of God's creation (no pun intended), I was in my absolute glory learning more about how science testifies to His masterful artwork. Not to mention, the *size* of that ark! Mama mia! There was so much to take in and ponder, I felt like a kid in a candy shop.

God's fingerprints were truly all over this trip. The morning we woke up to go to the ark, my sister (who was back home dog-sitting for us), texted me a picture of "the biggest rainbow she's ever seen," which silently screamed God's promises. Then, to further add to His sweet goodness, one of the family photos we took once we got there had a beautiful rainbow behind us. How fitting. No one could ever convince me that these rainbows weren't winks from our Heavenly Daddy.

I wonder how Noah must have felt when he saw that array of vibrant colors in the sky after 40 days of rainy gloom. On top of that, God told him this wonderfully radiant sight was set apart as a special symbol to represent His covenant with man. I'm sure this experience made Noah's faithful heart smile. It's neat to think about how even the science behind rainbows was created by God (it's also no wonder Satan has been trying to steal and redefine this work of art so aggressively, but rainbows are no more his than elephants are mine). Colossians 1:16 sums it up well, "For in him all things were created: things in heaven and on earth, visible and invisible, whether thrones or powers or rulers or authorities; all things have been created through him and for him." One thing I can confidently say, even after experiencing sexual identity issues myself in the past, is this: Regardless of how determined we do things, how loudly we state our feelings and opinions, or how strongly we feel about them, everything is still God's. Therefore, He's the only One who can set the standard of what's holy and what isn't. One day, we're going to have to answer for all of our actions here on Earth. He calls us to repentance simply because He loves us and knows exactly what's best for us.

In any case, getting to enjoy that time with my husband and kids was the greatest blessing of all because this trip happened a while after he and I had divorce papers prepared. Yet, there we were, together ... enjoying an incredible mini getaway as a *family*. The Lord knows how many vacations in the past weren't as good as they could have been due to us being at odds with one another. Saying He did a miracle in our hearts and in our marriage would be a very serious understatement! With that said, the little moments of laughter, random late-night snack adventures, and road trip chats with the kids, made the experience just as sweet and memorable as the attractions themselves.

I can't help but to think God's heart fills with delight as He watches us create lifelong memories that are only possible by His hand and His hand alone. Whether it's experiencing the grace of a restored marriage or the simple act of dancing in the kitchen with your kids, it's all made possible because of Him. Paul says it beautifully in Acts 17:28, "For in him we live and move and have our being." As some of God's own poets have said, 'We are his offspring.'

It's hard not to smile when I think about the joy He must feel when we truly appreciate all of these wonderful blessings He lavishes us with everyday.

· · ·

Reflecting back, are there any moments in your life when you just *knew* God was winking at you? How do these little reminders of His presence make you feel?

_____

_____

_____

_____

_____

Read the story of Noah's ark, while putting yourself in Noah's shoes. Journal your thoughts afterward.

_____

_____

_____

_____

_____

_____

_____

_____

_____

_____

_____

_____

_____

_____

_____

_____

_____

_____

_____

_____

_____

THIRTY-FOUR

" Greater Love Has No One Than This..."

Every year, around September 11th, I think of those who lost their lives due to the terrorist attack in New York City. To be honest, it's probably not healthy as I can sometimes get a little obsessive about watching survivor stories. This past year, one of the stories I listened to quickly turned my sad tears into happy ones. The story revolved around a group of firefighters who ran into a 59-year-old woman on the way down one of the staircases after their chief commanded them to evacuate. This woman couldn't continue down the stairs due to fatigue and encouraged the firefighters to keep going and save themselves. Rather than leave her behind, the six men made the courageous and selfless decision to stay right there with her—*no matter* the outcome.

Seconds later, the floors above them pancaked, and the tower collapsed. Once it was over, to their surprise, they were all still alive. This stairway (stairway B) was the only one left standing.

It was their sacrifice that spared their very lives that day because had they left her, they all would have died. Sure, this seems like the moral thing to do … especially for firefighters … but given our dog-eat-dog society, stories like this still stand out for a reason.

These men chose to stay with her as if she were their very own sister, mom, friend, or niece. Their racial, political, and other differences didn't matter at that moment. All that mattered was their compassion. Despite the darkness, the soot, and debris, light still found a way to break through. This is just one of so many stories of heroism from that day, but each one is uniquely different as it displays the true beauty of selflessness.

Simply put, it's no secret that our culture is self-seeking in more ways than I could ever fit into a book. Our selfish behaviors are symptoms of sin. We live in a fallen world.

This is one of the gazillion things that makes Christ so wonderful. Matthew 20:28 says, "Just as the Son of Man did not come to be served, but to serve, and to give his life as a ransom for many." Jesus coming into our dirty world, filled with the stench of sin, was a completely selfless act. Traveling from town to town in order to heal, restore, deliver, and teach us was selfless. Ultimately, laying down His life and resurrecting from the dead was the most selfless act of all, as it was the whole heart of His mission. In fact, He says in John 15:13, "Greater love has no one than this: to lay down one's life for one's friends."

Everything Jesus did, and everything He still does, is all done for our benefit. Thank God for our Savior who lives up to the title in a way we never could. The Father sent His one and only Son, just for us. What we *can* do, though, is learn from the example Jesus set and ask for His help in living out Philippians 2:3: "Do nothing out of selfish ambition or vain conceit. Rather, in humility, value others above yourselves." Yikes, isn't it so much easier said than done? Even so, it's possible, and we can get started today!

What heroic event made an impact on you, and what can you learn from it?

_____

_____

_____

_____

_____

How do you think you'd respond if you were put in a life or death situation that involved others?

_____

_____

_____

_____

_____

_____

_____

_____

THIRTY-FIVE

Fear is a Liar ... and Sometimes a Good Thing

One time, while cleaning the inside of my refrigerator, I decided to dump water into the spaces near the back (where I couldn't reach well). The plan was going very well as the water was coming back toward me, flushing all the residue out with it. Then, all of a sudden ... a giant black spider came rushing toward me in the stream of water, preparing to attack.

Like any normal person would do, I slammed the refrigerator door shut and screamed at the top of my lungs. Don't get me wrong ... I don't have a phobia of spiders, or any bugs for that matter (although, I would love to know what God was thinking when He created centipedes and millipedes).

I just don't particularly *like* spiders. Not to mention, I wasn't expecting my life to be threatened while cleaning the refrigerator—I was caught completely off guard! I vowed to leave the door shut until my husband came home from work. It simply wasn't worth the risk ... this task could wait.

A few hours later, my hero arrived home and opened the fridge. He took one look at the tarantula, picked it up and began walking toward me. Panic set in, *Here we go, he's going to tease me and pretend to throw it at me.* I braced myself.

"Is *this* what you were talking about?" he asked, while trying to keep a straight face. Hesitantly, I leaned in for a closer look at the eight-legged killer.

To my surprise, he was holding a plastic Halloween ring ... a *spider* ring.

How could this be? I could have sworn it was real! He practically jumped at my face! Okay, maybe that's a stretch, but still. I couldn't believe it. I delayed my cleaning mission and declared the fridge compromised all because of a *plastic* spider? How ridiculous. Where did that thing come from anyway?

I thought *wow ... If this isn't a silly, but accurate picture of how Satan works to exaggerate our fears, I don't know what is.*

He seeks, strategically, to magnify our fears even when they are absolutely unwarranted. Once we allow our brains to fill in the blanks of a situation and make it much worse than it actually is, it's not long before we lose our grip on reality even more. Our actions begin to follow, our faith gets weaker and the fear wins.

Thankfully, our Creator tells us over and over again in the Bible *not* to fear...

His heart is so very tender toward us. His beloved, fragile, and fearful humans. Like a parent, reassuring their scared toddler during a storm, He calmly bends down, cups our faces in His hands, and says, *look at me ... it's going to be okay, there's nothing to fear.*

Now fear can still be healthy and normal, of course. In fact, we know that God placed survival instincts within us (how wonderful it is knowing we can commune with this very same God).

Fear of God, on the other hand, is the most important fear of all. Proverbs 9:10 says, "The fear of the Lord is the beginning of wisdom, and the knowledge of the Holy One is understanding."

To fear God is to revere Him. We acknowledge that He is everything, and that apart from Him, we are nothing. Fearing Him means respecting His power, authority, and Word, while also knowing we can never truly comprehend the depths of His everlasting love for us. Fearing God is a manifestation of the belief that He is holy, perfect, and *just.*

Fearing God is essentially trusting God. It's knowing that the very breath within our lungs is only there because of Him. We should not take that gift and privilege lightly.

The more we know God's place, the more we know our place, and the more we know our place, the more we fear (and love) *Him.* And as our fear of God increases, the more we can recognize His truths and combat Satan's lies.

Lord, thank You for everything You are and everything You do. We love You so much.

Please help us put our fears in their proper perspective. You know more than anyone on this Earth what a wide range of fears we experience ... from fear of death, to fear of rejection, to fear of everything going on within the world right now. You care about the simplest, most common fears all the way up to the rarest phobias. Thank You for loving us so patiently and tenderly, even though we're undeserving of Your holy attention.

I pray for whoever is reading this right now. Only You know their heart, God, and the things that trouble them. I pray that you comfort their fearful spirits and reveal Yourself to them in a way that makes them feel safe under the security of Your wing. If there are deeper-rooted issues or unclean spirits at work causing their particular fear(s), please lead and guide them in understanding the reality of deliverance and all it entails. I pray You'll lead them to freedom in whatever ways You see fit, and that they'll give You the glory as they, one day, help others overcome the same fears they once faced.

In Jesus' name, amen

When you're completely honest with yourself, what is it that you fear? How can you begin surrendering this fear to God?

_____

_____

_____

_____

_____

Would you say you have a healthy fear of the Lord?

_____

_____

_____

_____

_____

_____

_____

_____

_____

_____

Consider writing the following verses on sticky notes and keeping them nearby. Put them somewhere you'll see them often (even your car would be a great place).

"God has not given us a spirit of fear, but of power, love and self control."

(2 Timothy: 1:7 ESV)

"Fear of man will prove to be a snare, but whoever trusts in the LORD is kept safe."

(Proverbs 29:25 NIV)

"I sought the LORD, and he answered me; he delivered me from all my fears."

(Psalms 34:4)

THIRTY-SIX

The Great Nurturer

There are a few things about this past Mother's Day that made it my most memorable one yet. However, one thing sticks out more than everything else: my son's crippled butterfly. About a month ago, we bought one of those live caterpillar kits from Amazon in which you can "grow your own butterflies." After patiently waiting for them to complete the process of metamorphosis, it was finally time for the newly emerged beauties to be released.

One butterfly, however, didn't fully develop like the others. We decided to name him "Ruffles" because one of his wings reminds us of the chip—well, the little part that's there, anyway. My son decided to keep and care for him during whatever time's left in the short life this little guy will live. He's been very diligent in providing him with adequate sunshine, food, and attention. Ruffles sat with us at the dinner table, his plate "full" as it included an entire orange slice and penny-sized piece of a strawberry. Then, he rode along with us to Big Lots, where he was pushed around in a cart (Happy Mother's Day to me!).

Watching my son love and care for this butterfly so tenderly, makes me think of our Heavenly Father and how sweetly He nurtures us. We're so fragile and dependent on Him, even when we don't realize or admit it. Just like we watched over the caterpillars as they went through a messy (and most likely painful) process on their journey to completion, God's eyes are always on us as we change and transform too. Furthermore, my son's scope of the world is so much bigger than his little one-winged friend could ever understand, and yet, my son still treats it compassionately—with kindness and respect. Sound familiar?

God doesn't only see *more* than we do, He literally sees (and knows) *everything*. Yet, in His great love and compassion, He not only treats us warmly, but He delights in restoring *our* broken wings. How blessed we are to be in His hands!

What daily aspects of God's provision and/or compassion make you feel loved and grateful?

_____

_____

_____

_____

Read the whole book of either Matthew, Mark, Luke, John, or Acts (or all the above). Choose your three favorite verses where you notice Jesus' compassion for others. Feel free to explore the old testament as well and highlight more areas where God was compassionate toward His people.

(Additional verses for further reading: Isaiah 55:8-9 and Psalm 8:4).

_____
_____
_____
_____
_____
_____
_____
_____
_____
_____
_____
_____
_____
_____
_____
_____
_____
_____
_____

THIRTY-SEVEN

Leopard Spots

While talking myself into getting out of bed one morning, my thoughts were interrupted by the words, "Can an Ethiopian change his skin or a leopard its spots? Neither can you do good who are accustomed to doing evil" (Jeremiah 13:23).

Just in case you're wondering if God was telling me that I might as well stay in bed because I do the world no good, He wasn't. But, I did hear those words audibly ... thanks to my audio Bible player, which continuously plays on low volume, right next to my bed. My body was still tired, but my spirit was wide awake and now causing me to ponder on that particular verse and the way it's often used in our culture. It's not unusual to hear, "a leopard never changes its spots!" or even "a zebra never changes its stripes!" This addresses the idea that "bad" people never change. Everyone seems to use the phrase, even if they're unaware it originated in the Bible.

Many believe some people are simply unchangeable, but there's *always* hope with God (Jesus says in Matthew 19:26, that with God, all things are possible). That passage in Jeremiah was in reference to the sinfulness of Israel and the fact that we cannot truly change without God's help.

Otherwise, to say people can't change is to say they can't learn and grow. Not only is that untrue, but it's an insult to our Maker as it rejects His capabilities and power. Personally speaking, I could never list the various and drastic ways He's changed me even if I tried!

Even the people society would deem as the most vile of the vile, such as former serial killer, David Berkowitz (also known as "son of Sam"), aren't beyond God's reach. The cross, along with the grace, mercy, and forgiveness it encompasses, was available to Mr. Berkowitz just as readily as it's available to anyone else. He humbly chose to receive Christ and now lives and breathes as a new man—no longer controlled by the demons that once held him bound.

When others only see the symptoms and manifestations of our deep-rooted issues and sins, God sees the full picture and chooses to love us anyway. I'm reminded of the song, *I am Your Beloved* in which the chorus says, "The One who knows me best is the One who loves me most." Those words get me every time, because the One who knows me best shouldn't love me at all! But yet, He does—despite my past, present, and future sins.

He loves you too … no matter what you've done at your worst, and no matter what ugly things are still lingering in your soul as you read this. This reckless, make-no-sense kind of love is one of the many reasons He's the only One who's able to redeem us.

The scriptures are filled with radical conversion stories. Surely, it's possible for people in our day and age to repent and begin new lives. It happens every single day! I love Paul's encouraging words in 2 Corinthians 5:17 (NKJV): "Therefore if anyone is in Christ, he is a new creature; the old things have passed away; behold, new things have come." Yes, this is still a process as we'll never be perfect or *completely* new on this side of life—but the beginning and continuation of this process is still possible, nonetheless. All we have to do is truly desire change deep within our hearts and allow for Heavenly help.

Considering this, God is an unapologetic, compassionate and *professional* Redeemer. A leopard doesn't change its spots because it can't ... but He *can*.

How can you better accept, embrace, and celebrate what God does in the lives and hearts of others (even if you have a hard time understanding at first)?

_____

_____

_____

_____

_____

Do you have a hard time believing people can change? Ask God to help you look at people through His eyes.

_____

_____

_____

_____

_____

_____

In what ways has He personally changed you? Were there times when you thought those changes were next to impossible?

_____

_____

_____

_____

_____

_____

_____

_____

_____

_____

_____

_____

THIRTY-EIGHT

Scream, Climb, Risk, and Love

As Jesus approached Jericho, a blind man was sitting by the roadside begging. When he heard the crowd going by, he asked what was happening. They told him, "Jesus of Nazareth is passing by." He called out, "Jesus, Son of David, have mercy on me!" Those who led the way rebuked him and told him to be quiet, but he shouted all the more, "Son of David, have mercy on me!" Jesus stopped and ordered the man to be brought to him. When he came near, Jesus asked him, "What do you want me to do for you?" "Lord, I want to see," he replied. Jesus said to him, "Receive your sight; your faith has healed you." Immediately he received his sight and followed Jesus, praising God. When all the people saw it, they also praised God. (Luke 18:35-43)

This bold and desperate man received his eyesight because he didn't listen to the people around him. He didn't care how he looked or what they thought of him … his tunnel vision for Jesus made him unstoppable and unable to be silenced. Due to his persistence, others ended up praising God too.

Let's look at another story…

Jesus entered Jericho and was passing through. A man was there by the name of Zacchaeus; he was a chief tax collector and was wealthy. He wanted to see who Jesus was, but because he was short he could not see over the crowd. So he ran ahead and climbed a sycamore-fig tree to see him, since Jesus was coming that way. When Jesus reached the spot, he looked up and said to him, "Zacchaeus, come down immediately. I must stay at your house today." So he came down at once and welcomed him gladly. All the people saw this and began to mutter, "He has gone to be the guest of a sinner." But Zacchaeus stood up and said to the Lord, "Look, Lord! Here and now I give half of my possessions to the poor, and if I have cheated anybody out of anything, I will pay back four times the amount." Jesus said to him, "Today salvation has come to this house, because this man, too, is a son of Abraham. For the Son of Man came to seek and to save the lost." (Luke 19:1-10)

Zaccheus jumped at the chance to receive this free grace, and he embraced this sacred moment—despite the crowd's opinion. Directly after the words, "the crowd muttered," are the words, "But Zaccheus stood up and said to the Lord." He kept his focus on Jesus, then he displayed evidence of a repentant heart! Isn't it just like Jesus to say, "let's have dinner at your place?" (my paraphrase). Running ahead and climbing that tree in order to get a glimpse of Jesus, resulted in hosting Jesus for dinner! Who would've known? We take a step (or in Zaccheus' case, a climb), and Christ gladly takes things a step further and sits with us!

This brings me to our next and final example— "the bleeding woman." Declared unclean, she was ostracized, dismissed, and financially broke. Yet, there was still hope, and it sure was promising. She knew, without a shadow of doubt, this one thing (one person rather) could effortlessly change her entire life in a matter of *seconds*. In other words, she knew that being willing to lose it all (her dignity and possibly even her life) would gain her everything ... if she could just pull this off.

Now when Jesus returned, a crowd welcomed him, for they were all expecting him. Then a man named Jairus, a synagogue leader, came and fell at Jesus' feet, pleading with him to come to his house because his only daughter, a girl of about twelve, was dying. As Jesus was on his way, the crowds almost crushed him. And a woman was there who had been subject to bleeding for twelve years, but no one could heal her. She came up behind him and touched the edge of his cloak, and immediately her bleeding stopped. "Who touched me?" Jesus asked. When they all denied it, Peter said, "Master, the people are crowding and pressing against you." But Jesus said, "Someone touched me; I know that power has gone out from me." Then the woman, seeing that she could not go unnoticed, came trembling and fell at his feet. In the presence of all the people, she told why she had touched him and how she had been instantly healed. Then he said to her, "Daughter, your faith has healed you. Go in peace." (Luke 8:40-48)

This woman's bleeding lasted 12 years prior to that one touch! I think she was past the point of believing she would ever be healed, and maybe even past the point of caring whether she lived or died. Nevertheless, there came that once-in-a-lifetime chance to chase the Hope down. In chasing Him down, she found healing and the bright new future she always wanted.

Perhaps there's something to be learned from these late, great brothers and sisters of ours, and perhaps there's something to be learned from Jesus. When we can't see, maybe it's time to scream as loud as possible. When we can't get a glimpse, maybe it's time to climb higher in order to change our perspective. When we want something bad enough, maybe it's time to risk our lives for it. And when it comes to choosing ourselves or others, maybe it's time to choose others.

Put yourself in each of these Bible characters' shoes. How do you think you'd respond in each of their situations if it were you?

_____

_____

_____

_____

If you were given the chance to ask these relentless saints any questions you wanted, what would you ask them and why? (Isn't it sweet knowing we *will* be able to chat with them one day in Paradise?)

Did you ever ask yourself what you'd be willing to lose in order to get closer to our Savior?

_____

_____

_____

_____

Read these full stories in scripture, and jot down any verses that the Holy Spirit illuminates.

_____

_____

_____

_____

_____

_____

_____

_____

_____

_____

_____

_____

_____

_____

_____

_____

_____

THIRTY-NINE

Ah, The Golden Rule...

The saying, "Treat others as you want to be treated," isn't used as often these days, is it? Although these beautiful, biblically-rooted words of Jesus are immensely powerful, it feels as if they're now collecting dust on a shelf somewhere—forgotten and unappreciated like an old toy. After all, they're in stark contrast to our current culture, as we want to live and act as we please but not be held accountable to (or mindful of) how we treat *others*.

In our fallen nature, we're all prone to be run by our own selfishness. I'll be the first to admit I could do a much better job applying this principle to my life. Doing our best to obey this commandment can make an impact on the world far greater than we could ever imagine. We will even see the ripple effects of our actions up close and personal one day in Heaven–our true and final home.

Trying our best to live this truth might look like putting ourselves in the shoes of the person holding up the line in the grocery store. Waving at her fussy baby, complimenting his shoes, or simply choosing to smile at the other person are ways we would all like to be treated if it were us. It's an unspoken way of saying, "I understand, and we're in this thing called life *together*." The simple beauty of human-to-human connection goes a long way. Perhaps you don't have much help with your own children, but you offer to sit for other parents so they don't feel alone, like you do. Although each of our circumstances vary, we should all try to give what we wish *we* had, to others.

Far beyond these seemingly surface-level situations, this commandment is meant to travel deep into our homes, churches, and personal circles. Every word Christ ever spoke was—and still is—golden, but these words He spoke in the sermon on the Mount became known as the golden rule for a reason. In fact, they were so important to Him that He says they *sum* up the Law. "So in everything, do to others what you would have them do to you, for this sums up the Law and the Prophets" (Matthew 7:12).

Here are a few questions that were asked of Jesus:

- "What is the great commandment?" (Matthew 22:36)
- "What is the first commandment of all?" (Mark 12:28)
- "What shall I do to inherit eternal life?" (Luke 10:25)

Jesus' answer remains the same in Mark 12:30-31.

"Love God with all your heart, soul and strength, (and) love your neighbor as yourself."

A golden answer to some commendable questions.

In verse 31, He goes on to say, "there is no other commandment greater than these." Love God. Love People. There we have it, folks ... a solution for mankind, once and for all! If only our lost and hurting world knew the profound power within these words. If only our world knew that there's only one, true living God worthy of our love. If only our world knew just how much He loves this planet and everyone who's ever been (and will be), on it.

When we treat others how we want to be treated, and love our neighbor as ourselves, it can help strengthen marriages, bring healing to fractured relationships, and so much more. A sense of peace and relief can flow freely when we operate in this spiritual way—for which we were created and designed. Even if it seems there's nothing to gain on our end, it feels so good when we do help others. It's our Daddy's heart in action, working through us—in the perfect timing and with perfect alignment—like a supernatural solar eclipse.

Write the following verses down, and place the paper somewhere you'll see it often.

"Jesus replied: 'Love the Lord your God with all your heart and with all your soul and with all your mind.'"

This is the first and greatest commandment.

And the second is like it:

"Love your neighbor as yourself" (Matthew 22:37-39).

Ask the Holy Spirit to help lead and guide you in treating others how you'd like to be treated, then begin applying what He reveals to you.

Journal some of the outcomes you've noticed that were a direct result of your choice to live by this golden rule.

_____

_____

_____

_____

_____

_____

_____

_____

_____

_____

_____

_____

_____

_____

_____

_____

_____

_____

_____

_____

FORTY

Don't Get Too Comfortable

Feeling productive one morning, I decided to reorganize my closet. This, of course, made me want to reorganize other spaces in the house too. Why not? I was on a roll. However, instead of actually organizing, I stood there and thought about how I needed (well, *wanted*) more wicker baskets and clear plastic totes. Before I knew it, I was making plans for both the closet and for my entire bedroom. Then, I remembered the words I often tell myself when I get in these reorganizing and redecorating moods. *Don't get too comfortable.*

God brought me to this house for a time and a season, and boy am I glad He did. Though living here provides a very tiny glimpse of country living, I'm in my absolute glory. It's music to my ears when I hear all the beautiful birds singing their sweet little hearts out. Not to mention, the grass is vibrant, the air is fresh, the people are down-to-earth, and the stars sparkle like a million diamonds. I've never felt more at home. Our Heavenly Father certainly knows what we need, and He knew I would relax well here during a time when rest was much needed in my life.

Even still, this peaceful sanctuary I've grown to appreciate is not my plan for long-term living. It's simply a sacred pit-stop before the next season. An eventual move, God willing, is always in the forefront of my mind. Therefore, everything I do around here, whether inside or outside, is centered around that move.

Don't get too comfortable.

I believe God wants us to take the same approach with our lives here on Earth. When we don't keep eternity in the forefront of our minds, we get too comfortable ... *dangerously* comfortable. Tomorrow isn't promised. We've become blind to the reality of our own fragility. Even as we sit in funeral services, it's almost as if we sit there in some delusional cloud of fog that subconsciously tells us we have more time left. And even if we do mentally put ourselves in that casket, it doesn't last long and often doesn't impact our spiritually careless ways of living. Sure, we may have some years left, but we can't say for sure. We simply *don't know*. Either way, the death rate is always 100% and whatever time we do have left is incredibly short in comparison to eternity. Realistically speaking, it's as if we have mere seconds left; we're all leaving this place at some point. The fact that our homes are cozy, our families are happy, and we own 10 cars or a house on a beach somewhere, makes no difference at all (1 Timothy 6:6-7). This speeding train cannot be stopped.

Paul tells us in Colossians 3:1-2 to set our minds on things above. "Since then, you have been raised with Christ, set your hearts on things above, where Christ is, seated at the right hand of God. Set your minds on things above, not on earthly things."

How we treat people, how we spend our money and time, how we pray, and how we view death, shifts dramatically when we learn to look at life through a lens of what's to come, rather than what is.

Heavenly Father,

Thank You so much for all You've given us here during our time on Earth. We are undeserving of all the wonderful ways You take care of us, and yet You still allow us the very blessing of life each morning. Help us to never take Your purpose for our lives lightly and please "teach us to number our days so we may gain a heart of wisdom" (Psalm 90:12).

In Jesus' name,

Amen

Read and meditate on the following verses. Ask God to help you consider eternity in all that you do and say. Of course, we won't get it perfect, but if anyone knows how to help us do better, it's Him!

    Colossians 3:23-24

    1 Corinthians 9:24-27

    2 Corinthians 4:16-17

    2 Corinthians 5:10

_____

_____

_____

_____

_____

_____

_____

_____

_____

_____

_____

_____

_____

_____

_____

_____

Acknowledgments

Thank you again for spending this special time with me. I hope and pray it's left you feeling closer than ever to your sweet Savior—He loves you so very much! May you keep your eyes on Him, and serve Him wholeheartedly as you embrace all that He has in store for you on this side of life.

Until next time, fellow soldier...

"What you are is God's gift to you. What you become is your gift to God."
    -Hans Urs von Balthasar

If you found this book encouraging, would you please be so kind as to leave a review on Amazon?

Embark on a transformative journey of faith and discovery with "*Eyes Upward*," a compelling collection of real-life stories written by Natasha Grantz, and woven together to illuminate the power of God's presence in everyday moments. With honesty, warmth, and unwavering faith, Grantz beckons you to look beyond the surface of your circumstances to experience deeper intimacy with God. Through these heartfelt anecdotes drawn from her personal experiences, she offers wisdom to navigate the many complexities of modern existence with faith and purpose.

From moments of doubt to triumphs of grace, each story serves as a testament to the transformative power of fixing your gaze upward—to Jesus. The thought-provoking questions and soulful contemplations will encourage you to pause and ponder on your own spiritual journey. Eyes Upward serves as a loving, down-to-earth nudge toward our gracious Savior.

Come along with Grantz on this six-week journey full of relatable, challenging, and occasionally humorous moments, as you're reminded to keep your eyes upward!

Natasha Grantz, a dedicated wife and loving mother, finds immense joy in life's simple pleasures. Whether she's fishing with her family (preferably saltwater), expressing herself through art, admiring nature's beauty, or simply tapping away at her computer, she does so with a grateful heart. Each of the many challenges Natasha has faced, deepens her adoration for her faithful Redeemer, fueling in her a desire to help others draw closer to Him too.

Often described as an "old soul," she generously shares the wisdom she's gained throughout those experiences—aiming to uplift and inspire those around her. For Natasha, writing isn't just a way to unwind; it's a therapeutic, heartfelt expression of love to her readers, and more importantly, to her Heavenly Father.

Natasha has written three additional books: A Changed Heart, The Culture Challenge, and her children's book, Do You Ever Wonder? Her testimony has been featured on CBN, and she has been a guest speaker at various churches and events. Currently, Natasha and her family live in a small town near Pittsburgh, PA.

Woven Books
YOUR STORY. HIS GLORY.

Also by Natasha Grantz

The C.U.L.T.U.R.E. Challenge

Do You Ever Wonder? (children's book)

A Changed Heart

If you found this book encouraging, would you please be so kind as to leave a review on Amazon?

Made in United States
North Haven, CT
21 December 2024

63213764R00134